WHERE PATHS MEET

WHERE PATHS MEET

PAUL ELLENBERGER

XULON PRESS

Xulon Press
2301 Lucien Way #415
Maitland, FL 32751
407.339.4217
www.xulonpress.com

Paperback ISBN-13: 978-1-66284-014-2
Ebook ISBN-13: 978-1-66284-015-9

For my Family

my wife, Florine, who walked tirelessly
beside me all these years
my four children and their spouses
my 13 grandchildren and their families
my great-grandchildren
and future greats

TABLE OF CONTENTS

Table of Contents

BACKGROUND

THE STORIES IN this book span over 100 years of ministry in West Africa. Most of the stories take place in the country of Guinea. Guinea is about the size of France, is bordered to the west by the Atlantic Ocean and has a population of 11 million. The country was created in the late 1800's as a colonial settlement between the French and the British. Guinea was a French Colony up until 1958 when independence was declared.

As is typical of many countries created during the colonial period, Guinea is home to about two dozen ethnic groups, several of which are mentioned in the book. The Fulanis, Maninkas and Soussous make up over 85% of the population. The primary languages spoken are French, Maninka, Fulani and Soussou. Maps have been included that provide an ethnic reference by geography, and identification of the cities in some of the stories. The primary religion in Guinea is Islam, however about 10% of the population is Christian.

Following the declaration of independence in 1958, the country was ruled by Sekou Touré until his death in 1984. During Sekou Touré's rule, the country was heavily influenced by the socialist policies of the Soviet Union and some of the ethnic groups experienced brutal repression. A military coup led by Lansana Conté took over the country following Sekou Touré's death. In 2010 the country held its first free election.

Guinea is rich in natural resources and is the second largest producer of Bauxite (used in the manufacture of aluminum) in the world. Guinea is blessed with abundant land suitable for agriculture, but the country has remained relatively impoverished with an average annual income per capita of $520.

A Diverse Ethnic Community

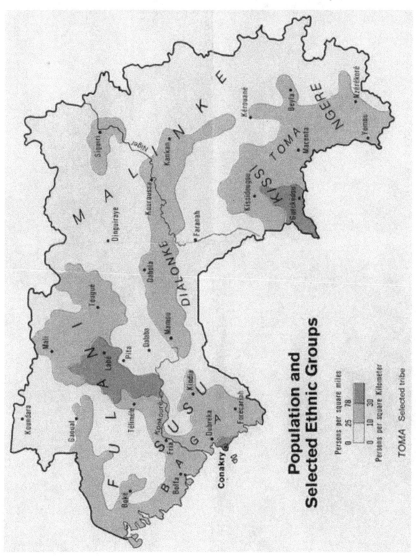

Population and
Selected Ethnic Groups

Guinea

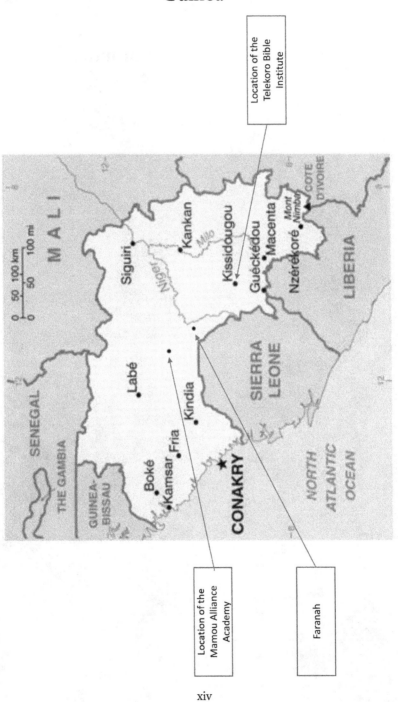

Location of the Telekoro Bible Institute

Location of the Mamou Alliance Academy

Faranah

REFLECTIONS

I HAD THE PRIVILEGE of working with Paul Ellenberger at the Telekoro Bible Institute in Guinea for twenty years. Our homes were in close proximity. This has given me a very good and fair idea of his life and character.

Paul is a special guy. He understood the local language and knew how Guineans thought and spoke. His knowledge of their culture was so profound and deep, that he was respected by everyone who knew him. He didn't "show-boat" that knowledge, but used it to help with decision-making. Paul also had a love for the Guinean people, and perhaps that is what set him apart from others. It moved people to confide in him, seek his opinion, and trust his judgment.

We spent hours talking together, standing on the path that separated our homes. Paul liked to talk about theology, and how biblical truth had impacted the lives of the students we were teaching. Our conversations often expanded to church and mission matters. Paul grew up on the mission field in Guinea, and the knowledge he gained from his experience gave him a clearer perspective than most. He had a unique understanding of where things were headed and how issues might be resolved.

In special meetings where palavers were being settled, one would always hope that Paul would be there because of his obvious expertise in cultural affairs. He was not overbearing, and he always listened to others, seeking a just solution to the problem presented.

There is no such thing as the "perfect missionary." But, in my mind, Paul Ellenberger was as close as they come. His desire for God's glory and the Guinean Church to succeed was at the core of his desires and he spent his life radiating Christ to both the national and international worker. Paul left a mark that will always be one of seeking to bring praise to the King. May his tribe increase!

Dave Harvey
Missionary Colleague and Friend

THE BEGINNINGS

MY DAD HAS always been a good storyteller. No one can tell a story like he can! As a kid, I remember my friends saying how interesting my dad was and how funny his stories were. I was like, "yeah, whatever!" I have come to appreciate his stories a lot more now that I am an adult. Every time I see my dad, I hear a new story and my mom often says, "Oh Sandie, surely you've heard that one . . . I've heard it a hundred times!"

For the last 15-20 years, family members and friends have been telling my dad he should write a book. He kept saying he didn't want to make a big deal about it or turn it into a book . . . he just wanted to write some stories for our family legacy. "We could type them up, mimeograph them, staple them together in a packet and pass them out to family members."

He started writing stories and last year I agreed to help him edit them and put everything together. Over time, I convinced Dad that his grandkids and great grandkids are probably not going to read a packet stapled together! He finally agreed to let us publish a book with his stories and I have enjoyed working with him the last year and a half on this project. We have spent many hours on the phone, clarifying, adding, changing, and tweaking. Dad has been very patient with me while I sought to make this book the best it could be. I have learned a lot about my grandparents and am deeply touched by the sacrifices they made for the sake of spreading the gospel. And I have a renewed appreciation for the work and ministry my parents had in Guinea.

I could not have edited and seen this book through to publishing without lots of help. My dear husband, Steve, was a great sounding board, giving wise advice on the editing and lending his calming voice when needed! He is responsible for the maps, background, back cover information and many rewritten sentences and paragraphs that greatly enhanced the stories. A simple thank you is not enough.

A big thank you to my son, Jason, for his invaluable help during the editing process. He brought a different perspective to the stories and his own set of unique questions and ideas.

A special thanks goes to my nephew, Paul, who spent many hours on the painting that would become the cover for the book. When I complained about how long the whole editing process was taking, he wisely said, "It takes as long as it takes . . . you can't rush these things, Aunt Sandie!" Thank you, Paul.

My sister, Karyn should get a medal for simply listening to me every single day for months and for supporting me through the whole process. I love you!

These stories may have been written for the enjoyment of our family, but I know that many others will want to read this book and will enjoy it as well. You will laugh, you will cry, but there will be no doubt about the truth of the gospel shining through these stories.

Enjoy!
Sandie Ellenberger Weise

KEY TERMS

C&MA   The Christian & Missionary Alliance, also known as the Alliance, the denomination we served and are a part of

MK   missionary kid

Furlough   now called "home assignment," one year spent in the U.S. visiting churches to encourage prayer and financial support

Term   the 4 years spent in Africa between home assignments

Bible School   Telekoro Bible Institute, Telekoro Bible School or Bible Institute

the mission   the local overseas Christian & Missionary Alliance (mission station – physical location of a ministry; mission vehicle – vehicle owned by the C&MA)

laymen   church workers and leaders that are not pastors

KRMS   Kabala Rupp Memorial School, boarding school in Kabala, Sierra Leone

ICA   Ivory Coast Academy, boarding school in Bouaké, Cote d'Ivoire

U.S.   United States

INTRODUCTION

AN OLD MANINKA proverb states, "The green leaves of the tree don't know that the dried and fallen leaves ever provided shade for anyone." Free translation: "Today's kids don't know that the old folks ever accomplished anything." Lest a new generation be tempted to think that my generation didn't do anything, I propose to set down these recollections.

I have four goals in view:

1. to record what family history I know
2. to preserve from my unique perspective an era of mission and church history in West Africa
3. to collect interesting stories and anecdotes
4. and, most importantly, to recognize and give testimony and praise to God for His intervention, guidance, provision and faithfulness in my life and ministry. To Him be the glory.

It is improbable that everything can be remembered, and that everything remembered can be usefully recorded. I confess that some of my recollection lacks documentation, but I intend to be as factual as possible while preserving what would be of interest to my readers.

Having lived in Guinea through 26 years of social upheaval, when one had to be very careful what was said or written, I wouldn't want to write anything that would bring harm or disfavor to the work of the Gospel or to the servants of Christ engaged in it. So, I approach this thoughtfully and responsibly.

"FOR ME, FOR ME"

ONE OF THE great Christian & Missionary Alliance pioneer missionaries in West Africa was Robert S. Roseberry. The last time that he returned to visit Guinea was in 1956, where he spoke at a field-wide, multi-ethnic conference. It was held under a large stick and palm branch shelter. I was one of four interpreters for his message. He was preaching from Galatians 3, and quoted verse 13. "Christ redeemed us from the curse of the law by becoming a curse for us . . ." Mr. Roseberry emphasized that Christ was made a curse for all of us, and then went on to make it very personal by underlining the fact that Christ was made a curse **for me, for me**.

As he continued with his message, I noticed that the interpreter next to me, Vieux Woro, wasn't following what was being said. Instead, he was striking his chest with his fist, repeating over and over, the words, "for me, for me." Tears were streaming down his face, and with each "for me" he kept sinking lower and lower until his face was on the dirt floor – "for me, for me."

That was the end of the preaching. People began sobbing and crying out all over that large audience, many crowding to the front to weep before the Lord, confessing sins and seeking the cleansing and power of the Holy Spirit. As a young missionary, I had never seen anything like it – a gracious, powerful moving of God's Holy Spirit across that African congregation.

THREE LIVES INTERSECT

THE YEAR WAS 1908. Clair had only finished sixth grade when he had to leave school and go to work to help support the family. He was the third of eight children born to a Pennsylvania coal miner, Henry, and his wife Lula. They were good solid Pennsylvania Deutsche, or German people, typical of the German settlers who came to this country in the 18th and 19th century. They settled in the Butler, PA area.

Earl, Clair's oldest brother, fought in the Spanish-American War under Teddy Roosevelt. Clair's older sister, Geraldine, died when she was 12 years old. Twin sisters Freda and Veda were born next, Veda only living a short time, and Freda outliving most of her siblings. Harold, Paul and Madele completed the family.

Clair found a job at a local grocery store delivering groceries to customers in the neighborhood. Later he worked in the meat section and learned butchering, a skill that would come in handy later in his life's work.

Clair had a best friend named Carl. They worked together at the same store, were of a similar family background, and often shared their thoughts on life and their aspirations for the future. They both attended The Christian & Missionary Alliance church in Butler and were looking forward to the annual missions conference. Missionaries from varying places in the world came to be part of the conference; it was a big event in their lives. The two young men loved the Lord and at one evening service, listened attentively to the message brought by the missionary speaker. They heard about what God was doing on the mission field and about the great need for workers to proclaim the

Gospel to people who had never heard. When the call was given to dedicate their lives for foreign missionary service, Clair and Carl felt greatly moved by the Holy Spirit, and both went forward eagerly to make this commitment.

In the weeks that followed, the two young men often got together to discuss what they would do. "We've made a commitment to God to be missionaries," they reminded each other, "and we must obey." They knew it would take a lot of money, and they didn't have any. But they felt so keenly the responsibility of their promise to the Lord that they finally came to what they felt was the only workable solution. They would both be missionaries, but they both couldn't go to the foreign field. One would go and the other would stay behind to earn money to support the other's missionary service.

It was Carl, a very shy, soft-spoken individual, who suggested, "Clair, you have the gift for preaching and for meeting people, so you go and I'll stay and support you." And that's the way it happened.

Although Clair hadn't finished high school, he was accepted at the Missionary Training Institute, now Nyack College, in New York. He studied under Dr. A. B. Simpson and graduated in 1916 at the age of 20. For his practical experience, he was sent to pastor a small group of people in Toledo, Ohio, a church now called The Westgate Chapel. His ministry supervisor was Rev. Isaac H. Patterson, pastor of The Toledo Gospel Tabernacle. It was there that Clair met Ruth, the oldest of Isaac and Mary Patterson's four daughters. She often came to play the piano for the young pastoral intern. It was there in Toledo that Clair and Ruth began a romantic relationship. Ruth later also attended the Missionary Training Institute in New York and felt God's call to serve Him.

The missionary call burned within Clair. During his time at the Missionary Training Institute, his commitment to be a missionary had crystallized in a call to go to West Africa. Alliance missionaries had been working there since 1890, in answer to Dr. A. B. Simpson's vision. Dr. Simpson is the founder of The Christian & Missionary Alliance, and his vision was to reach "the Soudan" with the Gospel. The Soudan was a vast tract of open savanna plains, extending across Africa, between the southern limits of the Sahara Desert and the northern limits of the equatorial rain forests. The plan was to follow the Niger River and establish a series of "gospel lighthouses" along its banks from its source near the Atlantic coast all the way to Timbuktu. Timbuktu was a renowned desert crossroad city, far in the interior of the largely unknown "Dark Continent." Many had already given their lives in the effort, and more missionaries were needed to take the message of Christ to those who had never heard the Good News.

Clair felt the urgency of his call; he **must** get to Africa to tell people about Jesus, and he must go as quickly as possible! He wrote letters and pleaded with the leadership of The Christian & Missionary Alliance, to send him. The fact that World War I was still raging did not deter him. Finally, in September of 1918, he was cleared to go. There were German submarines in the area and his ship had to return to port twice before finally heading across the Atlantic toward the west coast of Africa.

Guinea was closed to missionaries in the early 1900s and so most of them went to Sierra Leone first. There were attempts made to get into Guinea and many lost their lives to yellow fever. Clair served in Makump, Sierra Leone for several months before he was able to get into Guinea.

In 1919, ten years after Dr. Simpson's vision, Clair helped open the first missionary station in Guinea. The town of Baro was chosen because of its close proximity to the Niger River, and the Chief there was favorable toward missionaries. Clair worked with the Maninka people, learning the language as he went along. He often travelled by boat up the Niger River to evangelize.

Clair went back to the U.S. for his first furlough in 1922, and spent the second half of the year in France studying the French language. Upon his return to Africa in 1923, he left others to continue the work in Baro, and he moved to Kankan. Kankan was a large city and he felt there were more opportunities to reach people via the Niger River project.

In New York, Ruth had finished her schooling at the Missionary Training Institute. She and Clair had secretly gotten engaged before Clair left for Africa. In response to her call to missions, Ruth went to Guinea, West Africa in 1922. She started her language study in Maninka.

On November 2, 1923, Ruth and Clair were married in Makomp, Sierra Leone. French law at that time required parental consent for marriage until age 30. They didn't receive Clair's mother's consent in time, so they went to Sierra Leone to get married (under English control). Clair and Ruth Ellenberger were my parents!

Ruth joined Clair in Kankan and they continued to learn the Maninka language. They soon began translating the Bible into Maninka, starting with two of the most important books, Genesis and John.

Back in Butler, PA, Carl Hoffman had been able to establish his own business, Hoffman Auto Parts, which flourished under God's blessing. The store actually still exists today. True to his own missionary vision and promise, he sent money regularly to The Christian & Missionary Alliance to support Clair, and he continued doing so faithfully for many years until Clair went to be with the Lord.

Clair, Carl and Ruth were all faithful in their commitment to the Lord. They each used their unique gifts to serve Him, and they have gone on to their eternal reward.

Clair's first home, Bare, Guinea, circa 1919

Chapel where Clair and Ruth got married, Makomp, Sierra Leone, November 1923.

7

Maninka Translation Team in Kankan, circa 1925. Clair and Ruth on left

A FAITHFUL SERVANT

SAMORI TOURÉ WAS a religious Muslim reformer and military leader who resisted French colonial rule in West Africa. With a goal of Islamizing all of West Africa, he swept across West Africa and expanded from Bamako, Mali in the north to Sierra Leone, Ivory Coast and Liberia in the east and south. The French finally gained control of Guinea when Samori Touré was defeated in 1898. He was captured between Faranah and Mamou. When we would pass through the area, we could see the mountain where they said he was taken. Following the defeat of Samori Touré, the French intensified the colonization of West Africa.

The French wanted young men to be educated in the French language so they could be translators and go-betweens between the local chiefs and the French administrative authorities. Some of the young men who normally would not be given an opportunity for education were chosen to learn French. Many of the leaders from favored classes, the chiefs, the blacksmiths and the sorcerers,[1] didn't want their sons to go away to study the French language. They wanted them to stay at home and learn the family business. So, others were chosen instead.

There was a young man named Cova who was from the Macenta area. He lived in the small village of Malima, in the heart of the Toma tribe. He was small and puny and "wouldn't be a good help on the

---

[1] In the New Testament, the word "sorcery" was primarily applied to divination (speaking to spirits) and spell-casting, because sorcerers used their incantations to conjure occult power. It is an attempt to bypass God's wisdom and power and give glory to Satan instead.

farm," so he was one of those chosen to be sent to the schools the French opened. He did his primary schooling in Macenta and was sent to Kankan for his secondary education in the late 1920s. He was then hired by a Frenchman as a clerk in his store in Kankan.

My parents, Clair and Ruth Ellenberger, were stationed at Kankan at the time. They met Cova because his roommate was their house helper. Cova would get off work and come and sit on our porch, waiting for his friend to finish the dishes so they could go home together. My dad found out that Cova was educated in French, so he gave him a French New Testament. Cova read the New Testament, until he became so convicted that he hid the book under his clothes in his trunk. But since he had little else to read, he would eventually dig it out and continue reading. He would be overcome again with conviction, and would hide the book once again. This went on for some time until he was finally convinced that God's Word was the Truth. But before he became a believer, he wanted proof! He had learned about prayer, asking God for something. So, on several occasions he prayed to God for something specific. Once it was about lost keys to the Frenchman's store, and he found them. Another time it was about his health. His answered prayers moved him to become a believer in Christ.

But Cova became troubled by the darkness and the lost condition of his people, and he went to one of the missionaries and asked, "Is there no one who can go to my people and tell them the Way of Life?" Cova offered to quit his job and to accompany the missionaries when they were available to go to his people.

Harry and Grace Wright were early missionary pioneers. They started a new ministry in Faranah, but found it difficult to gain acceptance in the community. The local people viewed them as outsiders. One day, Harry went hunting down by the Niger River and shot a hippo. He hired a man with a dugout boat to help him retrieve the dead hippo. But the hippo stuck its head up and Harry had to shoot it again! He wound up bringing two dead hippos back to town and presented them as a gift to the Chief. From then on, Harry and Grace Wright were well accepted!

By 1930, the Wrights had finished building the mission station at Faranah and were ready to start a new work elsewhere. They agreed to go to Macenta and Cova planned to accompany them. He gave up his position at the French store, but not without difficulty. The Frenchman offered him salary increases, a better position, etc., and couldn't at all understand Cova's reasons for quitting. Cova just had to go and tell his people the Good News of salvation in Jesus Christ.

In Macenta, the Wrights found a hut to live in, but since they had no authorization from the French government to hold religious services, they just played the pedal organ and people crowded in to listen. The first convert was Kissi Kamara, who had served in the French military and had killed many people. He found forgiveness through Christ for the blood of the ones he had killed and was filled with God's peace.

The Wrights moved to a two-room place where one room was the bedroom and the other room was dining/living room/classroom/chapel! Many people came to faith in Christ at their new home. Over the next months they built a chapel that seated 200.

Harry and Grace had to leave Macenta for health reasons, and the ministry was left in the hands of Cova and Pastor Woro Sumaoro. Cova married Tolo, establishing the first Christian family among the Toma people. Cova started a preparatory training school and mentored many young men, encouraging the best students to go on to the Telekoro Bible Institute.

Mr. Roseberry, the chairman of the mission, made a trip to Macenta and Cova acted as his interpreter and house helper. "Nothing was too menial," Mr. Roseberry reported. "I never had a better servant or a more faithful interpreter than Cova." They went to Malima, Cova's home town, where they were given a hearty welcome. Cova led the service there and they visited many villages where they preached the gospel.

Cova acted as a pioneer evangelist. As far as I know, he was never a pastor as such. He was human, had some problems, but he loved the Lord with all his heart, and he was faithful to the end. He introduced the Gospel to his people, the Tomas, to the Kpelees, another large tribal group and also to many others. In Cova's later years, the church in Macenta had a room for him behind the church hall.

The last time I saw Cova was at the National Church Conference in Guéckédou in 1989. The church was brimming full with delegates from all over. There was a section for extra seating beside the church, covered with palm branches for a roof, and wooden planks on cement blocks for seating. Cova sat on the plank in front of us, taking it all in, enjoying the worship and praise. I remember thinking, "This is the man who is largely responsible for all of this!"

The Lord used Cova to spread the gospel from Macenta to N'Zérékoré and beyond. And he has his reward!

13

A BOYHOOD BUDDY

IN THE EARLY 1930s, our family lived in the town of Faranah. My dad started a church there and had a preaching and teaching ministry in Faranah, as well as in the surrounding villages. We didn't have a vehicle at the time, so we walked everywhere. My mom spent time in the nearby village of Modiya, teaching Bible classes to the young women. Mom sometimes rode in a rickshaw, drawn by a strong young man. The ministry was difficult and discouraging at times. Faranah is a strongly Muslim area, and the people were not receptive to the gospel.

My parents found a village about 28 kilometers from Faranah, that was more open to the Gospel. It was a village of the Yalunka tribe, called Yatia. My folks worked with a few local Yalunkas to help them translate Bible portions, Christian lessons and songs in the Yalunka language. It was easier to work on this material at Yatia, where there were no interruptions, and where they could talk to and minister to the Yalunka people. Eventually we built a house and a chapel there so our family could spend periods of time at Yatia, especially during the dry season.

The first convert from Yatia was an ex-military man called Sergeant Bokari, who had five wives and a growing family. Many of them also confessed their faith in Christ, including Bokari's mother, Nga Nansaba. Bokari's oldest son from his first wife, was Sayon. He was three years older than I was, but we became good friends.

Sayon was good with a sling shot, and he taught me how to make them and use them. He was the best shot in the village and I was the next best. We spent hours each day tramping through the fields and brush, shooting birds, lizards, snakes, mice, or whatever. A number of smaller boys followed us around and were charged with looking for the right sized stones for us to use.

Usually Sayon got the first shot, but I remember once getting the first shot at a monkey and hitting it right between the eyes. It fell down from the tree, and I went dashing over, yelling, "I shot a monkey!" But before I got there the monkey came to and took off!

Sayon also taught me about using a sling, like the one David used to kill Goliath. That one is harder to use and I needed lots of practice. I remember practicing using my sling when I was away at boarding school. I was down a road where nobody was ahead of me. But my stone went behind me instead, and there was a woman with her young boy coming down the road. I yelled, "Look out!" but just then my stone bounced off the boy's head, and he collapsed.

I was in deep trouble, especially since the boy's head was bleeding. Mr. Kurlak, our boarding school director, had to talk for me at the unavoidable palaver. He had to agree to a certain payment to get me off the hook. Fortunately, the boy didn't suffer any complications.

Sayon became the leading hunter in his region, with a rifle, that is. He was called to various districts to get rid of leopards that were attacking the people's cattle or the hippos that would ravage the rice farms.

Florine and I returned to Guinea as missionaries in 1955 and we lived in the town of Faranah. We did evangelism work, preaching and teaching in the surrounding villages and we had the opportunity to see Sayon frequently. In 1988, when our son, David, and daughter-in-law, Heidi came to Guinea to introduce us to our first grandchild, Kristen, we were able to stop at Yatia and see Sayon again. But the big meeting that day was when my first son, David, met my friend Sayon's first son, Dauda, or David!

People who live in the African interior are used to creeks, streams, rivers, and some ponds. They have seen these streams and rivers overflowing their banks and spilling into the fields during the rainy season.

But they have only heard about the ocean, a water that is so big, you can't see across it.

Sometime in the early 1980s, I heard that my buddy Sayon had finally come to Conakry where we were living. I just had to get in touch with him. "Sayon, have you seen the ocean?" I asked him. "Yes," he answered simply. "Have you really seen the ocean?" I insisted. "Yes, it's out there," he said without much enthusiasm. I said, "Get in the car."

We lived in a house right on the Atlantic Ocean with a gate opening out onto a long sandy beach. I took Sayon out there, he kicked off his sandals, and the first wave washed over his feet. The second wave washed over, and he stuck his finger in the water and put his finger in his mouth but didn't say anything. The third wave came, and he did the same thing, tasting the water and saying excitedly, "It's true, it's true. It's salty!"

All I could think of was Psalm 34:8, "Oh, taste and see that the Lord is good! Blessed is the man who takes refuge in him!"

I learned some time later that Sayon had drifted away from his faith. If God, through his grace, could restore someone like Manasseh,[2] who led his people away from God, he certainly could have restored Sayon's faith. I hope that I will see him in heaven one day!

---

[2] Manasseh was one of the kings of Judah. See II Chronicles 33:9-20 to read his story of repentance and God's forgiveness.

THE RUPPS' LEGACY

ONE OF THE most important concerns for missionaries abroad is the education of their children. The growing number of missionary children on the field of French West Africa presented a real challenge regarding their education. The Rupps were missionaries in Sierra Leone and they felt God was impressing on them to start a school. The parents could give their full attention to the ministry of the Gospel if their children had a school to attend.

In answer to this need, David and Grace Rupp, along with their two sons, Kenneth and David, came to the city of Mamou, in Guinea, with the vision to start a school. In 1928, The Mamou Foyer was opened. Children of missionaries came from all over West Africa: Ivory Coast (now Cote D'Ivoire), Soudan (now Mali), Upper Volta (now Burkina Faso) and Guinea. The school later came to be known as Mamou Alliance Academy.

I came to Mamou in 1931 to begin first grade and David Rupp Jr. was my first roommate. We were the only boys at the school that year and there were at least three girls, Helen Loose, Ruth Roseberry and Erma Powell. The Mamou school children called David and Grace Rupp "Uncle and Auntie Rupp (pronounced Roop).

The Mamou Foyer was located in downtown Mamou on a corner property next to the Catholic mission and was within walking distance of the Mamou train depot. A small classroom was built behind the large, spreading house, which used to be an old hotel. The wide veranda was a handy play area during the rainy season.

The veranda was large enough to hold church services when the public was invited. I remember once when Pepe, a local Christian, died and his funeral was held there. We had to line up and file past his wooden casket to pay our respects. To our great surprise, his eyes were wide open, and it took a long time to erase Pepe's staring at us from the casket!

By 1936, we had 19 students and we were starting to outgrow the original Foyer. A site for a new school was selected on a hill outside of Mamou, and construction began. The original compound became the "Old Foyer" and the school was moved to the New Foyer in 1938. Many of the Mamou children had made pledges toward the building of the new school, and Uncle Rupp, who rode his bicycle out to supervise the work, would give us a progress report on the construction.

One of the necessary features of the New Foyer was a well that would furnish water for the school. The well had to be dug by hand. One day a passer-by, himself a well-digger, stopped to peer down into the well. His well-digging tool fell off his shoulder and landed point-first on the head of the man at the bottom of the well. The children joined in prayer for him and rejoiced when he recovered. Light for the digging process was furnished by a mirror held to reflect the sunlight to the bottom of the well. Water was struck at 100 feet. The large roof area of the main L-shaped building also collected rain water. It was channeled into a water tower and a cement catch basin underneath the back entrance to the building.

It's interesting the things children remember! Auntie Rupp used to sneeze quite loudly and distinctively **"ha – ba – shoo"** and you could hear her all over the compound. In the evening we would be playing hide-and-seek, prisoner's base, or other running games. Auntie Rupp would finally call out, "Now, children, it's beginning to get cool, you better get your sweaters on." Sweaters in those days were made of wool and pulling a wool sweater over sweaty arms was something we did not look forward to doing. To this day I don't like sweaters!

The time spent at the dinner table was often used for education. Proper behavior, chewing with your mouth shut, chewing each mouthful forty times, obedience, and kindness were just some of the things we learned. And the Bible memory work that we did has stayed with me all these years.

When Uncle and Auntie Rupp wanted to communicate with each other at the table, and didn't want the kids to hear what they were saying, they would say it in Timne, the first language they learned in Sierra Leone. They also spoke Kuranko, a language from both Guinea and Sierra Leone. But they couldn't speak Kuranko in front of the kids, because some of us could understand that!

Uncle Rupp did a lot of walking and riding a bicycle. He was always trim and muscular. During the long school vacation (December–April) the Rupps would often return to Sierra Leone to continue ministries they had been involved in before coming to Mamou. Sometimes they ministered in other areas of Guinea. Often Uncle Rupp would travel long distances on his bicycle. He quoted one missionary kid as saying, "Uncle Rupp, you were made to travel on those roads in Kuranko country with your bicycle. My daddy was made to use the auto!"

I remember Uncle Rupp as a tireless witness for Jesus Christ wherever he went. He reminded me so much of my own dad in that way. Nothing would keep them from stopping to tell someone about Jesus, and the bicycle made that much easier!

The Rupps loved "their children." Once when Uncle Rupp returned from a trip to the Mamou Foyer after school was already in session, he wrote of his arrival and being greeted by the kids. "What a happy crowd the children were! To fully appreciate it you would have to come and see [for yourself] the school in full swing." And in his report for the school year 1935, Uncle Rupp wrote that "the angels in heaven were made to rejoice with us four times when four little boys and girls received Christ into their hearts as their personal Savior this past year."

The Rupps returned to Sierra Leone after WWII and God gave them a new vision to start another MK school. The school was located in Kabala, Sierra Leone and named Kabala Rupp Memorial School (KRMS). Aptly named! When Mamou Alliance Academy closed, a few of the remaining students, including three Ellenberger children, went to KRMS. And that's another story!

David and Grace Rupp's two sons, Kenneth and David, later returned to Sierra Leone as missionaries and ministered for many years to the Kuranko people. A granddaughter, Edie, and her husband also labored for years in Sierra Leone. And a great-granddaughter, Dawn, and her family spent a number of years ministering to the Yalunka people in Guinea, neighbors of the Kurankos.

The Rupp's ministry positively impacted the lives of many MKs and allowed many West African missionaries to minister in remote areas without having to worry about the safety or education of their children.

God bless David and Grace Rupp.

Students at Mamou School, 1931. David and Grace Rupp, center, Ken and David Rupp, right. Paul, front row right.

Early Mamou students, Paul back center

FIRST NIGHT AWAY FROM HOME

I T WAS APRIL, 1931. I was six years old, and this was my first day at the Mamou Foyer. Uncle and Auntie Rupp were the house parents, and Miss Sigler was the school teacher. The Rupp's younger son, David, was my roommate. He was a lot older than I was and left for the U.S. after that to complete his high school studies.

That first night away from home is etched in my memory, especially when it came to bedtime. That was like 7:30 p.m., earlier than I was used to, and I was all alone in the room. Auntie Rupp prayed with me and tucked me in under a tall, white mosquito net. Before she left and shut the door she said, "Now, Paul, don't get out of bed."

As I lay there looking around and not at all sleepy, I happened to feel that my heart was beating very slowly. I knew that when running around playing, it would beat much stronger than that. Now it seemed to be getting slower and slower, until I was afraid that it might stop. I couldn't let that happen. The only way I knew how to get it beating faster was to run. But the lady said not to get out of bed. So, I ran in bed, down to the foot and back to the pillow, back and forth, until my heart felt that it was doing better. Now I kept track, and when the heartbeat got slower, I would repeat the running process.

This happened two or three more times until Auntie Rupp heard the squeaking bed springs and came to see what was going on. When I told her that my heart was going to stop and made her feel for herself, she explained to me how the heart slows down to rest at night while we sleep and that it wouldn't stop. That's how God made it, she said.

Then she told me about my heart, how Jesus loves me and needs to come into my heart and make it clean for Him to come and live there.

It wasn't that night, but later that first year at Mamou that I really understood about my spiritual need and gave my heart and life to Jesus Christ.

THE LORD WILL MAKE A WAY

with input from my sister, Dorothy Emary

IT WAS SEPTEMBER 1, 1939, at the Mamou Foyer. My sister, Dorothy, my brother John, and I were excitedly awaiting the arrival of our parents, Clair and Ruth Ellenberger. They were coming into Mamou by train that evening. Our family was scheduled for furlough in the U.S. and would be leaving soon. But that very same day Germany invaded Poland, and that marked the beginning of what became known as World War II. The next day, September 2, France and Britain declared war on Germany. And so, for those of us living in French West Africa, the war was on.

Our parents realized that all our travel reservations would now be invalid, and they decided to return to their station at Faranah, planning to wait until school was over in early December to make the trip to the U.S. They figured that the initial travel crush caused by the onset of the war would be over by then and there might be a better chance for foreign travel.

As an early teen, I was greatly disappointed because our lost travel plans had included the transatlantic crossing from France to New York on the French ocean liner, *SS Normandie*, the largest passenger ship afloat. And how I was looking forward to that!

For the next three months, life at the Mamou Foyer settled into the school routine. The war seemed a long way away, but it had some noticeable effects on us. Shortly after the war began, Uncle and Auntie Rupp, our house parents, were called in by the local police because of their German name. We pronounced it "Roop" and the French knew it as Rupp, like "up." They weren't arrested, but the French were wary of them and kept them under surveillance.

Another thing that changed very quickly was the availability of sugar. Sugar in French Africa was all imported from France, so with France now at war, shipping priorities changed. We were faced with eating our morning oatmeal or "foni" (a locally grown cereal something like cream of wheat) without sugar. That's when locally produced honey came to the rescue, and although it took a little time to convert our taste, it was better than the alternative!

The war brought another innovation to life at Mamou school called victory gardens. We each, or together with another student, had a garden bed for which we were responsible. The produce from the gardens, if there was any appreciable amount, was to supplement the vegetable diet for our meals. It made us feel that we were having a small impact in alleviating some of the distress caused by the war.

School closed in early December 1939, for Christmas vacation, and our family prepared once again to try and make it to New York. With no reservations possible and ship schedules mostly non-existent, this seemed to be a daunting consideration. Mr. Burke, the French business agent in Conakry, who helped the Mission with travel arrangements, advised our parents to remain at Mamou until he notified them by telegram that he had shipboard accommodations for our family. Our parents prayed about this and felt that we should go on to Conakry anyway and be ready when a ship came with cabins available. After all, there were only two trains weekly from Mamou to Conakry, and it could be possible to be informed of an available passage and not be able to get to Conakry in time to make it. Mr. Burke wasn't too happy to see our whole family arrive in Conakry.

We spent our time in the capital at the Grand Hotel. Every evening our family would walk down to the beach from the hotel. We would look out across the Atlantic Ocean toward the west and north, about where New York would be, nearly 4,000 miles away. We would form a family circle, hold hands, and sing together this little chorus:

I know the Lord will make a way for me,
I know the Lord will make a way for me.
If I live a holy life, shun the wrong and do the right,
I know the Lord will make a way for me.

Dad would then pray, asking the Lord to make a way for us to get to New York, and we would return to the hotel. We did this each evening. Suddenly, here was a ship with two empty cabins, two bunks each, and just right for our family. God had indeed answered our prayers. Apparently, the cabins were empty because at the last port of call, another family couldn't board as their passports had expired.

The ship, the *Tagliamento*, an Italian freighter, could accommodate up to 14 or so passengers without having to have a doctor on board. It was on its way to its home port of Trieste, Italy, making stops along the western coast of Africa for lumber and other cargo. We would have several more stops before we reached Genoa, Italy, where we could presumably get passage to New York.

We finally set sail mid-December 1939. Our first port of call was Dakar, Senegal, and we spent most of a day there. My dad went to the market to look for people who spoke the Maninka language of Guinea, so he could share the Gospel of Jesus Christ. He did this everywhere he went. He was talking with a group of men when we heard our ship's horn, and we tried to convince Dad that we had to go. He said it wasn't time yet, that the captain had given a later time. Soon the port agent appeared, to hurry us back to the ship. The gangway was already lifted, and all but the bow and stern lines were taken in. We were lifted to the deck in a chair connected to a crane!

We had some precious cargo with us onboard the ship. My folks were tasked with hand-carrying the original manuscript of the Maninka New Testament to the U.S. for printing. My mom, along with other missionaries, had spent years working on this translation. It was wrapped in tar paper, a waterproof type of paper, and then placed in a bag, which we kept in a specific location in our cabin. My sister and

I knew where the manuscript was located and the two of us were in charge of retrieving it in case we had to evacuate onto the life boats.

Two days out from Gibraltar, my brother John was coming down the ladder from the top bunk when the ship rolled, and he fell and broke his arm. It was a compound fracture with the bones visibly out of place. Dad picked him up, and said aloud, "Lord, help us," a characteristic prayer of his in every situation. He jerked the arm bones back into place and put the arm under running water in the sink. The ship's purser was called and brought splints and bound up the arm. When we arrived at Gibraltar, Dad took John to the hospital where the arm was x-rayed and found to be set perfectly in place. They only had to put the arm in a cast, and he spent the night there at the hospital. John was there for their Christmas Eve party and was given a toy aircraft carrier, made in Pittsburgh!

When our ship was brought into the port of Gibraltar, we were at the rail to watch the pilot come aboard. To our amazement, he fell off the rope ladder into the water and had to be fished out. We learned later that he'd had a heart attack and died. Our ship was to be the last one he was going to bring into port before he retired. How sad that was! Our stop in Gibraltar was primarily to refuel, with coal! What a messy job! Our family was able to go ashore and do some sight-seeing, including visiting an ancient Moorish castle.

On Christmas eve they had a dance in the captain's dining room. The tables had been unbolted and moved, to provide room for dancing. Dorothy remembers that the captain came and asked her to dance. He said he had a daughter just her age! Dorothy felt so badly that she had to turn him down, but she didn't know the first thing about dancing!

There were many ships in the harbor at Gibraltar, including warships. At night the non-combatant ships were all lit up and we could see their country's flag painted on the ship's side, which was also illuminated. Our ship had large Italian flags painted on its sides since Italy was still a neutral country at that time. French and British ships, however, were completely blacked out at night. I remember watching one of Britain's largest battleships gliding past us in the moonlight on its way out to sea.

Our ship spent several days in the port of Valencia, Spain, to unload cargo. The Spanish civil war had just ended, and there was a lot of destruction visible from the port. After lunch one day, I gathered all the little loaves of bread left on the table, stuffed them in my pockets, and went up on deck to chew on the bread and flip some pieces to the sea gulls. I noticed a young boy and girl, barefoot and wearing tattered clothing, wandering on the dock near our ship. I thought they might be hungry, so I said "Hello" to them in Spanish and showed them the bread. They made no move or response, so I threw one bread down to them. The little girl went and picked it up, realizing then what it was, and began to dance excitedly. I decided they needed the bread more than I or the sea gulls did, and I finally got the little girl to come over by the ship and she held her skirt out while I dropped in all the bread-sticks I had left. They seemed happy as they hurried away.

It was getting a lot colder, so when our ship docked in Marseilles, France for several days, our parents bought us warm jackets and coats. Also, at Marseilles, the French police removed several German passengers who had boarded the ship back in Cameroon, in Equatorial Africa. We didn't see them again. The trip from Marseilles to Genoa, Italy, was an overnight run, they said, but we hit a raging storm just as we put to sea and for four days, they could only keep the bow of the ship heading into the mountainous waves. The whole bow would disappear under the water and the screw (propeller) at the stern would come out of the water and spin, making quite a noise. Every day at the dining table the steward would say to us in his Italian accent, "Tomorrow Genoa."

By the time we arrived in Genoa, Italy, our passports had expired, but the port authorities let us debark and go to a hotel on the promise that we would get new passports at the American Consulate there in Genoa. We spent ten days in Genoa waiting for a ship to New York. It was cold, the coldest winter in 50 years, they said. Outside the hotel there was a large icicle hanging from the second story to the sidewalk, apparently from a broken pipe. There was no central heating anywhere, so we kept warm by wearing our coats and visiting museums and places of interest, like the birthplace of Columbus. I also remember seeing some of the Italian Fascist Party's Black Shirts marching in the city of Genoa. We went down to the port one day to see the American passenger ship, the *SS Washington*. We admired the huge American flag painted on the side of the ship and enjoyed the music played by the on-board band.

Finally, we were able to leave for New York on the large Italian passenger liner, the *SS Conte di Savoia*. We made one stop in Naples before heading west. Our family explored the museum there in Naples while others did an excursion to Pompei. Mt. Vesuvius, an active volcano just five miles from Naples, was plainly visible with its plume of smoke in the background. Back on the ship, we passed the Rock of Gibraltar and out into the Atlantic Ocean heading for New York. Our ship was like a cruise ship, so we had wonderful meals. Mid-morning appetizers were served on deck and mid-afternoon tea and small cakes were served.

On February 1, 1940, one day after my fifteenth birthday, the *Conte di Savoia* plowed through the ice chunks in the Hudson River to its berth in mid-Manhattan. This had been an emotional, but also enjoyable experience for me and my family. At last . . . New York! Six weeks after leaving Africa, we were finally passing the Statue of Liberty.

SS Conte di Savoia, with the Rock of Gibraltar in background

31

A LEGACY OF
PASTORAL EDUCATION

WWII DISRUPTED THE ministry of missions in French West Africa, but it did not stop it. Missionaries in the United States on furlough (now Home Assignment) were not able to return to their work on schedule. Women were not allowed to come back into the country because of the war, so my dad returned to Guinea alone in 1942. My mom and two brothers were delayed in the U.S. for the time being.

Dad long believed that the missionary alone could not accomplish the mission of reaching the world for Christ. He felt there must be the calling and training of local pastors and teachers to effectively spread the Gospel to all in need of God's saving grace. Back in the 1930s, Dad and Mom held several short-term Bible school sessions at our Faranah station, with some students coming from the forest country. Unfortunately, rice-planting time always interrupted those efforts.

My dad felt God was moving him to start a Bible School. He had a deep desire for a full-term training facility to be located in the forest country, from where the majority of the future students would be coming. The people in the forest country were pagans, mostly animists, and were much more open to the gospel than those who lived in the north, mainly Muslims. So, Dad traveled across Guinea, looking for prospective students, adults who had a desire to study God's word and take the gospel to their world.

After months of preparation, Dad and his team finally opened the new school in May, 1945. My mother and younger brothers, John and Ralph, had finally been able to return to Guinea. They joined my dad for the inauguration of the Telekoro Bible Institute, located just outside the city of Kissidougou.

The Bible School was for training church pastors and leaders and encompassed a four-year curriculum with a year of practical training between year two and three. The curriculum was in the Maninka language. In a country of many different languages and dialects, Maninka was considered the "trade language," or the market language. And Maninka was the first language in Guinea to have the whole New Testament. But students had to be taught how to read and write before deeper exposure to Biblical truths. My parents were among the first teachers at the school. Those early days must have been very challenging.

Adult students, married and single, came from several different tribal areas to fulfill the vision of building the church of Jesus Christ. This Bible School was the first place in Guinea where members of different tribal groups found themselves living together. The tribal animosities were forgotten, and they became a "family," a forerunner of the intertribal church.

Thatched-roof buildings with mud walls provided a classroom, a chapel, and living accommodations for the students and the missionary teachers. Eventually, more permanent structures were built, including a beautiful chapel that was named after my dad, "The Ellenberger Memorial Chapel." A planned campus lay-out featured a large central square with a mown lawn dotted with flowering shrubs. The campus later became a draw for visitors. Even the governor of Kissidougou would bring his visitors for a drive around the Bible Institute campus to see what he called "The Garden," the prettiest sight he had ever seen!

My dad went to be with the Lord in 1950, but my mom stayed on at the Bible Institute. Earl and Peggy Stewart headed up the staff, and my sister, Dorothy and her husband, Howard Emary, came to be teachers. Florine and I came to the school to help in 1961, and we eventually became permanent faculty members.

We witnessed a lot of changes at the Bible Institute over the years. I was the last missionary Director of the Bible Institute. In 1967, a Guinean pastor was named by the Guinean church to direct the school. We saw the school's instruction transition from the Maninka language to French, a collegiate educational level added to the program, and the first women to join the regular course of study in French.

The men who graduated from the Institute during the first few years served as laymen and leaders in the local churches. Florine and I felt very privileged to be part of the first ordination ceremony in 1956. These men were sent out to pastor churches and plant new churches. We saw the impact the Telekoro Bible Institute was having on the growth and health of the Church in Guinea. To God be the glory.

Original thatched-roof Chapel, Telekoto
Bible Institute, circa 1945

35

Clair with students at Telekoro Bible Institute

Ellenberger Memorial Chapel, Telekoro Bible Institute

Our family home, Jelekova Bible Institute

Graduating Class, with Paul Ellenberger and Dave Harvey, Telekoro Bible Institute

40

Students going out "two by two" to preach in surrounding village

Paul teaching, Telekom Bible Institute

NOT THE SEABEES!

IN 1941 MY dad was the speaker on a missions tour in California. There he heard about a special branch of the U.S. Navy that was being formed to help the war effort, the Seabees, from C. B., or Construction Battalions. This special Navy division was conceived to build roads, bridges, airports, military bases, storage facilities and whatever else needed to be done to help the war effort and to hasten the ending of WW 2. Many older men with construction, machine shop, mechanical or other industrial abilities were enlisting in this new Navy branch.

When my dad returned from California, he brought a Seabees brochure and gave it to me. "Paul," he said, "it doesn't look as if this war is going to be over before you graduate high school, and you will be obliged to serve your country in one way or another. I found this brochure of a new organization of the Navy that focuses more on construction and service than on fighting and killing, and I thought that this would be more of a help in preparing you for the future."

I took the brochure, and there on the front were these sailors in dress blue uniforms lined up with their rifles at "parade rest." Yes, I thought, just what I wanted! I had crossed the Atlantic Ocean by ship for the first time when I was only three years old and at least four more times after that, and I liked being on board ships. So this looked like a great possibility for me. Then I opened the brochure at random, and here were those sailors, now in dungarees and down in a ditch, digging with pick and shovel. I closed the brochure and handed it back, saying, "No, Dad, this is not for me. This is not the kind of Navy service I envision!"

After that, I did look into the U.S. Navy V-12 program for Navy officers' training for high school graduates, but my vision without glasses wasn't good enough for the V-12 program. So, I opted for the A-12 program for Army officers' training. I gathered the needed documents and recommendation forms. After graduating high school, I had to join the group going to Detroit for induction into service, and, wouldn't you know, I forgot my special papers! When our bus arrived at the service center, we were given instructions about how to proceed. Those with special papers were to go one way, the rest the other way. I told the man that I had forgotten to bring my papers. He said, "Sorry, Mac, you go over there with everybody else."

It was a long day in a perpetual line of men going from one physical or verbal exam to another and just waiting for the guy ahead of you to finish. Finally, I arrived at the desk of a man who stamped my paper with a two-word stamp: Army – Navy. And he asked me, "Which do you want, Mac, Army or Navy?" I responded, "Well, the Navy, of course." And he said, "Sit down, sailor." I couldn't believe my ears.

The guy at the desk tried to engage me in conversation as he finished the work on my papers. "Where would you like to go?" he asked. And I answered, "On board a Navy ship, of course." And he said, "Well, you'll be on a ship but only to take you to where you will serve." My reaction: "I'm not in the Navy?" "Yes, you're in the Navy," he replied, "but you're in a special branch of the Navy; you're in the Seabees." All I could see was the picture in that brochure with Seabees in dungarees digging in a ditch with pick and shovel! I told the man at the desk, "I don't want to be in the Seabees. Please change me over to the Army." He said, "I can't do that. You're in the Navy now." I asked to see the officer in charge, who told me the same thing. I was almost in tears, but I was now in the U.S. Navy Seabees. And I was eventually very glad that I was. Dad was right! And God certainly had His hand in all of this.

BOOTCAMP AND BEYOND

MY BOOT CAMP training began at Camp Peary, Virginia, near Williamsburg, in July 1943, and things were bound to be different for me. We were issued dungarees and dress blues and all that goes with being a sailor. And there were things that I had to get used to, like coffee, for instance. I had never even tasted coffee before. My folks didn't drink it, and the only thing we were permited was "preacher's tea," hot water with milk and sugar. Now at Camp Peary it was hot coffee for breakfast and iced coffee for lunch and dinner. I had to use four or five spoonfuls of sugar to get the coffee down. The water was too chlorinated to drink. I got used to drinking my coffee that way until the war ended and we returned to the U.S. and learned that sugar was rationed. So I stopped using sugar in coffee and on cereal, and haven't used sugar since.

Our 119th Naval Construction Battalion (NCB) was commissioned on August 14, 1943, and we left four days later for a month's "advanced training" at Camp Endicott, Davisville, Rhode Island. We finally reaching Camp Lee-Stephenson at Quoddy Village, Maine, for a three-month tour of duty. We were assigned to work details for construction and repairs, a foretaste of what was ahead for us. Winter found us there in Maine, and I remember my night-time guard duty outside with the temperature at 20 degrees below zero. We also had sessions of training with fake wooden rifles out in 24 inches of snow on the ground.

But we were spared the whole winter there in Maine. Right after Christmas we boarded trains bound for California. We lived on the train for six days before arriving at Camp Rousseau, Port Hueneme, California, northwest of Los Angeles. We spent six weeks of preparation for overseas duty.

Finally, on February 21, 1944, we boarded the *USS West Point*, a refitted cruise ship formerly called the *SS America*. It was painted in camouflage and sailed alone, due to its ability to sail fast and outrun the Japanese subs. 8000 troops and 400 Army nurses were aboard ship for the trip to New Guinea in the South Pacific. After two months of temporary duty in Australian New Guinea, we were taken to Hollandia, Dutch New Guinea, where we spent the next ten months. Our battalion was stationed near Lake Sentani, and this turned out to be not far from where the Alliance Mission headquarters is now located.

Across the wide valley toward the island's interior was the prominent Cyclops Mountain Range and its beautifully visible waterfalls. Shortly after our arrival I joined a small group of buddies who wanted to trek through the jungle and get a closer view of the Cyclops Waterfall. While passing the time in our pup tents[3] that night with a candle for light, a winged termite flew in around the candle, just like the ones we used to roast and eat as kids in Africa. I grabbed it, tore off its wings, and roasted it in a spoon over the candle flame, and ate it. My buddies were horrified, and long after that episode they still called me "Bugs." The next morning, we arrived at the top of the falls, and we had to cross over the stream in order to get down off the mountain. The rushing current was strong, and a couple of the guys were afraid to wade into the current, so I got in the water, braced myself against a rock at the very top of the falls, and helped these buddies over. The fellows all recognized the danger of what we had just done, and they asked me to offer prayer and to thank God for His help in getting us safely across the falls. My brother, John, told me that more recently a missionary was washed over those same falls and killed.

---

[3] a small canvas tent used for shelter, light enough to carry in a backpack

My Company A was detached from the main camp at Sentani and was located at Tanah Merah Bay, some 25 miles away, to construct eleven 10,000 barrel steel fuel storage tanks. This was to become a refueling center for ships. My job was as a "corporal of the guard" with the security detail for the project. I drove a Jeep to post and inspect my guards where the large tanks were being built. The Jeep had no brakes, but I had no problem gearing down to come to a stop. Then a Lieutenant borrowed it one day and went over the bank with it. The jeep soon had new brakes installed!

A lot of our mates at the main camp thought of us as being out in the jungle, but actually we lived very well. Our cooks visited ships refueling in the bay and traded Japanese flags and other souvenirs the men collected, for steaks, chops, fancy desserts, etc., not typical military fare.

After the construction of our refueling center was completed, we moved to the main camp, where the rest of the construction projects had also been completed. We didn't have much to do while we awaited our re-assignment to the Philippines. There was a mountain stream that came down and passed near our camp, and someone had the great idea of using one of our bulldozers to push a dirt dam across the stream at a good place in order to produce a swimming pool. Unfortunately, the stream kept pushing holes through the earthen dam, and the water would disappear. I happened along and suggested that because I was in charge of the stock of tarpaulins on the base, I could get a couple of tarps which we could use to line the earthen dam and then use bags of sand to cover the tarps and reinforce the dam. A buddy and I had to do the underwater job of placing the sandbags, but this worked marvelously. Soon this swimming hole became a famous pool frequented by personnel from the Navy, Army, WAC, WAVES, and the American Red Cross.

Paul with his mom after Boot Camp, Flint, MI, 1943

THE PHILIPPINES

IT TOOK FIVE landing ship tanks (LSTs) to carry our 119ᵗʰ NCB and our equipment from New Guinea to the Philippines. As our ship entered Manila Bay, we could see the explosions of the fighting still going on in Cavite, where a US Naval base was located, and eventually captured by Japanese troops. We passed between Corregidor Island and then toward the mainland of Luzon Island, where Manila is located.

When our LST beached, our Skipper came on the intercom to announce that all hands were to be secured to the ship until further notice, but as soon as the big doors opened and the gangway was lowered, we went off to explore Manila. I was one of a group of five or six guys that left the ship. In a pile of rubble near the ship one of the guys saw a nice boot and started to pick it up. But there was a foot in the boot – a dead Japanese soldier. We moved on, going into the city of Manila. Soon we were stopped by an Army MP officer. "Where are your shirts?" he demanded. "What's it to you, Mac?" one of our number replied. None of us wore shirts. In New Guinea we never wore shirts. The MP asked, "What outfit are you with?" "The 119ᵗʰ Seabees," was the answer. "Oh, Seabees," the officer said, and he turned and walked away. We were now in the middle of the city of Manila, and the only ones without shirts! We didn't do that again.

Our battalion was settled in tents in a large mango orchard just as the mangos were ripening. Our cooks thought this was great and prepared mango salads and desserts for us. I loved it, but our men didn't know what mangos were, so they didn't even want to try them. They completely ignored our chefs' interesting efforts. That stopped the mango menu but I was still able to get mangos from the locals and enjoyed them all by myself!

The major tasks of our battalion in the Philippines was first clearing rubble, and then building roads, camps for military units, storage facilities and other construction projects. My job on arrival at Manila was on the "honey wagon" or garbage truck. We took the large garbage containers to the shore of Manila Bay and dumped the stuff in the bay. By the second or third time, we found a group of locals waiting for us with pails, pots, pans, and containers. One man's garbage can be another man's dinner! I remember one man with his arm in the slop all the way up to his armpit. His hand came out with a big steak which he shook and stuck in his container, a big grin on his face.

When the Japanese took over the Philippines, all of the Americans were placed in prison. They were eventually released when the U.S. troops invaded. Shortly after our arrival in Manila, I heard about some missionaries that had been held as prisoners in New Bilibid prison, south of Manila, and I determined to go and see if any Alliance missionaries were there. But since we worked seven days a week, I had to wait for a day off. I got the driver of the honey wagon to drive me down to the New Bilibid prison, only to find out that all the freed captives had been taken to Santo Tomas prison in Manila.

I had to wait for another day off and went to the prison in Manila. I found that all the Alliance missionary prisoners had been repatriated to the U.S., except for Ralph Bressler Sr., who had been a missionary on one of the other Philippine islands. He seemed happy to meet me and was very grateful that I came for a visit. He invited me to have lunch with him there. The military had set up a food line for these who were still at the prison. Mr. Bressler had several empty food cans which he filled with food and brought back to transfer to the mess kits so we could dine together. He told me about his son who was wounded when the U.S. Army freed the prison at New Bilibid. The boy hurried to find shelter when the gunfire erupted, but the bullet caught his foot as he went around the corner of the building.

After my stint on the honey wagon, I was put on a construction job which I liked and which was, as my dad had said, a good training for the future. But one day a guy from my tent came back bragging that he had passed a rugged driver's test that the rest of us couldn't, and telling us that he was now driving for the Transportation division. He kept bragging about his great ability, so I finally went to Transportation and signed up to take the driver's test. This test turned out to be speeding the truck, a 10-wheeler dump truck, through its six forward speeds and then stopping the truck within a given distance without using the brake. This is what we did in New Guinea with our jeeps, so I had no problem and passed the test. I told my tent-mate that he wasn't that great a driver, that even I had passed the test. I thought that I had properly squelched him and was glad to get back to my construction job. A couple of days later, on the daily overhead announcements, we heard, "Ellenberger, report to Transportation." So . . . I became a truck driver.

One of my jobs as a truck driver was hauling sand, rock, and gravel for different construction sites. There were three or four of us, and we liked to travel closely together in convoy, passing through local villages by "gearing down," racing the engine to change gears and making considerable exhaust noise. Everybody knew who the Seabees were! Later my job changed to driving a truck with a boom on the front, that used the winch cable like a crane to move equipment and materials on the job site or from one job to another.

Las Pinas, Philippines

52

GOING HOME

V-J DAY, SEPTEMBER 2, 1945, announced the end of our mission, but it took some waiting to get back to the U.S., or as we said, "going home." The older fellows went first, especially those with 44 points needed to be discharged. I didn't leave Manila until early December 1945, on the big aircraft carrier *USS Hornet,*[4] the whole hanger deck of which was fitted with bunk beds. I chose the top bunk so that if any of the guys got seasick, I would be above the inevitable. I had a bad rash that covered my body, and which the saltwater showers on board didn't encourage me to use.

We arrived in Seattle early one morning with hardly anyone on the dock to meet us, contrary to the news we had heard about ships arriving in San Francisco and being escorted by boats with water cannons spraying a welcome. Getting out of Seattle proved to be a problem. There was only one train a day to Chicago, and a long line of travelers, mostly service personnel in uniform like us. We got to the gate just as the train was declared full. My buddy, Merton, had an aunt who lived in Seattle, and we spent the night at her house. We got up real early the next morning in order to be at the front of the line to wait for the train that wouldn't leave for Chicago until 5:00 p.m. It meant that all day long we had to defend our position from people who tried to crash the line.

Sometime during the morning, I went to the ticket window to get some information about my train schedule getting out of Chicago.

---

[4] The *USS Hornet* is famous because it is a museum in Alameda, California.

There was a girl ahead of me who apparently didn't get a good reply about her travel plans. When she left I asked my question at the window, turned to leave, and noticed the girl still there. "Did I hear you ask about Flint, Michigan?" she asked. "Yes," I replied, "that's where I'm headed." "Oh," she said, "come over here. I have a proposition for you." She had accompanied her sailor husband who had just shipped out of Seattle, and she was on her way home to Flint, Michigan. But because all the service personnel had priority, she probably couldn't get out of Seattle before Christmas, which was two days away. The guy at the window had just told her that her only chance of getting out of Seattle now was to pose as one of these serviceman's wife. "So, would you be willing to let me pose as your wife?" My answer, "I'm one of a group at the head of the line that doesn't want anyone crashing in, so I'll have to ask the others, and if they agree, I'll be happy to have a wife."

My buddy, Mert, a big burly fellow, was the boss and had kept the line free of intruders. "Yes," he said after a moment's reflection, "it would be good to have a woman in the group." So, this girl – and I can't even remember her name – joined our group. And I will say that she brought a liveliness to the group that made our long trip a lot more interesting. At the gate for departure, she told the ticket man, "I'm his wife." And the man looked at me, and I said something like "What am I supposed to say?" And he let us go through. Of course, we stayed together in Chicago where we had to transfer to another train going to Flint. We arrived in Flint around 3:00 am, and her parents met the train. They took me to their home until a more modest time when her dad drove me over to my grandmother's house. And it was the day before Christmas!

BEST APRIL FOOL'S DAY

CHRISTMAS WAS THE beginning of my 30-day leave. My sister, Dorothy, also lived with my grandmother and my Aunt Jessie, and it was such a relief to be in the U.S. and not have anything to do. I made a trip to Wisconsin to visit my buddy, Merton. That was up near Lake Superior in January, and they only had an outhouse!

After my leave ended, I had to report to Navy Pier, Chicago, where we didn't have much to do. I thought I had enough points to be discharged because my rating was Machinist Mate 3rd class CB rating, but this rating in the regular Navy was frozen, so the points didn't count. I tried arguing this point, but the Navy must have thought otherwise. When my name came up on a duty list for San Diego, California, I did get a sympathetic response when I pointed out that I was from Flint, Michigan, and that I would soon qualify for discharge. Instead, they sent me to Grosse Ile Naval Air Station, near Detroit. There I was assigned to Transportation and put in charge of the vehicle tires and tire repair for the station, with two German PWs working for me. These PWs liked it when I brought them a newspaper to read; I guess they could read English OK. And I tried to bring them treats now and then. After all, they did all the work! Since my office was there beside the base dispatcher, I could opt for any interesting runs he might have.

Once a high Navy officer's body was to be buried in Arlington National Cemetery and had to be in Washington, DC, by a certain day and time for the burial ceremony. His coffin with the body was sent from Grosse Ile Naval Air Station in a military ambulance which broke down on the way. By the time the driver could call in, the time was getting tighter, so the dispatcher called the base Captain to get his permission to use the Chevy ambulance. It was the only base ambulance that didn't have a governor, or speed control. He asked me to make the run. What a great feeling, speeding down Fort Street in Detroit with siren on and flashing red lights going. I should add that I made it to the train station in plenty of time.

The time finally came for my discharge from the U.S. Navy Seabees. We arrived at the huge Great Lakes Naval Base, and a group of us were trying to find our way. Along came a young Navy officer, an Ensign. Just out of habit, as Navy personnel who had spent two wartime years overseas where saluting anyone was not a priority, we all looked the other way, attempting not to notice an approaching officer. He stopped near us and said in a loud hard-to-ignore voice, "Doesn't anybody salute officers around here?" We turned and looked at him, and gave him a forced salute. Of course, we wouldn't want to be arrested just before our discharge.

And we finally got our discharge papers, dated April 1st, 1946. The best April Fool's joke ever!

But I still had an issue to resolve. When I entered the Navy, I tried to be like the guys, like everybody else. And this led me away from the Lord and from living a life of trust in Jesus, and I regret that I wasn't the Christian example and witness that I should have been during my time in the Navy. After my discharge, I realized that I couldn't continue on like this, that God had a real claim on my life that I couldn't ignore. I repented, asking God for His forgiveness and returned to following the Lord with all my heart. I didn't need to be like the guys, but like Jesus. My life had been transformed, my desires changed, and I felt a real joy in my heart. I rededicated my life to God to love Him supremely, to live always for Him, and to serve Him with my whole heart.

Paul Ellenberger, US Navy Seabees, 1943-1946

A CALL TO MISSION

WORLD WAR II was over, and I was finally discharged from the U.S. Navy Seabees in April 1946, after almost three years of service. I had to re-commit my life to the Lord and come to a decision of what I wanted to do with my life. College seemed the logical choice, and I was now covered by the GI Bill.

Wheaton College was the Christian school that I knew about, and my application was accepted, except for the following year, 1947. When my sister, Dorothy, heard about my disappointment and that I couldn't wait for a whole year to begin college, she said, "Why don't you go to Houghton College with me?" My reaction was, "Houghton College, where's that?" It was in Houghton, New York, south of Buffalo, and my sister had already done her freshman year there.

Houghton College accepted my application for the fall of 1946. Those first days, three years after graduating from high school, were hard. But I eventually got back into the habit of studying and learning, and actually enjoying it. Since I was three years older than my classmates, I felt more pressure to decide what I would do upon graduation.

The Missionary Training Institute (MTI) in New York, now known as Nyack College, conducted a large annual assembly at Rockefeller Center in New York City. It was called a "Congress of Bands." Each "Band" had a prayer group that represented a different area of the world. I learned about this big annual meeting and felt that the Lord was leading me to attend it.

On a Friday afternoon after my last class, I left Houghton in my '36 Chevy. I was prepared to drive all night in order to be at Rockefeller

Center the next morning for that assembly. A big snowstorm that night complicated my travel, and New York City received a record 14.7 inches of snow, but I was still able to arrive at the Center in time.

The program included messages given by a Nyack MTI student for each of the world geographical areas. Africa was represented by a young lady, Judy Ryan, an MK from Guinea. God used her message to speak to my heart. The service ended with a call to come forward to commit your life to missionary service, as God would lead.

Because I was in the upper balcony, I was asked to come to the front of the balcony. There I made my commitment to be a missionary to Africa, and from that time forward my life was dedicated to God and to His service. This commitment would be an important factor in my choices, my decisions, and my life's work.

MKS ARE UNIQUE

WHEN I WAS nine years old, my family came from Africa to the U.S. for our furlough year and settled in Flint, Michigan, where my mother's parents lived. The day we moved into our rental house, I came out and stood on the sidewalk in front of our home, looking over my new surroundings. A boy about my age from the house next door came out to talk to me. I don't remember all that was said, but this neighbor boy must have heard some things about me. He seemed to know I was from Africa and thought I spoke with an accent. He suddenly said, "You're a little furiner." And he punched me in the face. He apparently didn't like the way I talked and considered me a foreigner! And I thought we spoke the same language!

The MK – missionary kid – is different! But MKs are also Americans, and that's why we are also known as TCKs – third culture kids. We were born and/or grew up in a different country and then came to the U.S. with our parents every fifth year for furlough, now known as "home assignment." We are from one culture, coming to another culture, but actually forming part of a third culture.

I'm sure things are different now, but when I was growing up, coming to the States to finish high school or begin college could be challenging. For instance, you might need a drink and the drinking fountain was right there, but you had never used one before. So, you had to stand there and watch one or two others use the fountain before you could figure out how to make the water flow. And, of course, you were too embarrassed to ask someone.

When I was a freshman at Houghton College, I was one of the few students with a car, a well-used 1936 Chevy sedan. For Christmas break, I drove back to my grandmother's house in Flint Michigan. I had a full car, including my sister, Dorothy, and four other student friends who were also going to Michigan for Christmas.

We cut across Ontario, Canada, and arrived at the Michigan border from Canada. The officer asked me where I was born, and I said "Africa." He asked about my citizenship, and I answered, "American." My sister, Dorothy, gave the same answers. The girl sitting beside her answered, "India." The officer then went to the car's back window, and the two sisters sitting there responded "China." And finally, the third passenger in back, a young man, responded with "Indonesia."

Amazingly, the officer let us proceed, and I immediately jumped Bill about his answer to the officer. "You were born in Ohio," I said. "Why on earth would you ever say something like Indonesia? That could have gotten us in real trouble." Bill replied, "Hey, I can't sit back here and be the only one not born in a foreign country!"

MKs and TCKs grow up having all kinds of experiences that the normal kid here in the U.S. doesn't have. Yes, I consider us to be "advantaged" and wonderfully unique!

VILLA IMMANUEL

IN FEBRUARY 1954 Florine and I, with our seven-month-old son, David, left the U.S. to go to France for language study, before we could head to French West Africa as missionaries. We crossed the Atlantic on the British liner, Queen Elizabeth II, with its delightful English ambience. We were served afternoon tea with pastries and scones every day on beautiful china.

We lived in southern France during our one year of French language study, at the Villa Emmanuel in Mornex, France, just across the border from Switzerland. Villa Emmanuel was a Christian farm that catered to vacationing tourists, mainly French, but also Swiss, English, German and now American. I would be studying at the language division of the University of Geneva.

Madame Stocker ran the place and her daughter and son-in-law also lived at the Villa while preparing to go to the mission field in Africa. They had twin daughters, Trudie and Erna, who were a year older than David. They liked to play with him, and after he began walking, they would hold his hands and walk with him. So cute.

While at the Villa we attended a small French Reformed Church in Mornex that was within walking distance. The first Sunday, we were sitting there enjoying the pastor's sermon. David wasn't fussing or crying, but he was cooing, making "baby noises." The pastor stopped preaching and said, "Would somebody please take that baby out." I understood that much French, so I whispered to Florine, "The baby is bothering the preacher." Just then an elder came and Florine got up and left with David. The preacher went on. But pretty soon he stopped again and said, "Will the lady with the baby please take him out. He's still bothering me." Florine had been standing in the small entryway because it was raining. When she saw the elder coming toward her again, she hurried out with David and walked home in the rain, pushing him in the carriage.

The pastor apologized to me after the service, but said he just couldn't concentrate on his sermon. I don't think we took David back to the church again. The French didn't take their babies to church, and they didn't have a nursery. It was a good lesson for me in later years on how important it is to include children in the church.

During our time in France, Florine stayed with David at the Villa and was tutored in French by one of the women who worked there, while I attended the University of Geneva in Switzerland. I rode to the University on a borrowed bicycle, until the return trip up the mountain to the Villa got to be too draining. So, we bought a little Renault 4 car, much like a VW Bug, and that proved to be a God-send. We were able to get around more easily and go shopping in Geneva at Au Grand Passage, the big department store that had escalators.

David was always pretty quiet and well-behaved, but his eyes were sharp and he was inquisitive. One day he noticed the red button at the bottom of the escalator, and he pushed it, which stopped the escalator! Store employees were running around trying to find what the problem was, and David stood there quietly with his hands behind his back, looking amazed and innocent.

Before moving on to Africa to begin our missionary service, we took a trip through Switzerland, Germany, Holland, Belgium, and Luxembourg, returning to the Villa down the east side of France. This was February 1955, and winter. David had the back seat of our little Renault to himself, and, in spite of the fact that the heater didn't work very well in this rear-engine vehicle, he looked quite warm and comfortable in his yellow snowsuit. We had to spend one night in the car at a mountain pass where the snow plow couldn't clear until morning. Good thing we had blankets with us!

We visited a bear den in Germany. It was just this hole in the ground and we could look down into the hole and see the black bears down below. We also enjoyed seeing beautiful old buildings that had been built over 200 years before, with their gothic architecture. In Holland we saw gorgeous flowers in window boxes. They looked like a post card.

The trip was very relaxing and gave us much needed rest before we started into the next chapter of our lives.

Queen Elizabeth II, 1954

65

Florine with David, Switzerland

66

Paul, Florine and David, Villa Immanuel

BABY CHICKS

THERE WAS A conference to be held in Bouaké, Côte d'Ivoire. The political situation in Guinea had not been good for some time and visas were hard to come by. For the first time in several years, I was able to get visas for five of our Guinean pastors to leave the country and attend this important conference. There would be pastors and lay leaders from all over Africa. The conference was a great blessing and a real eye-opener for these Guinean pastors, whose contacts had been restricted.

Coming from a country with limited commercial access, my pastor brothers went on a shopping spree, so that when we boarded the plane to return to Guinea, they were loaded with carry-on stuff. One pastor who was going up the steps to board the plane, had purchased a large galvanized bucket. It was so full that he had to put it up one step at a time!

I used the opportunity to purchase what I could never find in our country . . . several dozen European baby chicks. I was taking them home to raise for egg production. At the door of the plane, the French stewardess saw my cardboard carton with holes in it, and she exclaimed, "Oh, you have a baby kitten!" "No, Mademoiselle," I said, "It's not a kitten, they're baby chicks." And her incredulous response was, "Really? Baby chicks!" Well, I put them under the seat for the trip, and they chirped all the way. But then, the full plane wasn't a very quiet place anyway!

When we arrived back in Guinea, we had to go through the police check and customs, but my brother pastors were home and knew how to take care of themselves. I, on the other hand, had a problem at customs. The official asked me for a certificate of origin for the baby chicks. I had to admit that I didn't have one and didn't know that one was necessary. I explained that the chicks were for me and some of my missionary friends. They were for our personal use and we would not be using them for profit. The official said that I still needed a certificate and that without it he would have to confiscate the chicks.

I tried all the excuses I could think of, but I knew he was just pushing me to give him money to let me go. I thought of the possibility of just wringing the necks of all the chicks and then letting him have them, but I realized that would not be a proper solution. I didn't have the necessary papers, and he wanted some money to fix it. I still had some French money from Côte d'Ivoire, about $6.00 worth, that people in Guinea prize more than their own currency. The customs officer readily accepted that and let me go with my baby chicks.

And that's the African way!

A BIBLE FOR DR. GALENA

D R. GALENA WAS a neurologist from Russia, who worked at the large government hospital in Conakry, the capital city of Guinea. I first met Dr. Galena while accompanying a missionary for a consultation with her. Several months later, I was at the hospital to see a young lady from our church who had been gravely ill and in a coma. I found Dr. Galena, who was examining our patient. The doctor had recently arrived back from her vacation in Russia.

She looked up, acknowledging my greeting with a nod and a smile, and kept on with her examination. When she finished, she came over to me, shook hands, and said quietly, "Pastor, could I speak with you for a moment?" "Of course," I replied, "please feel free." She said, "Oh, not here. Let's go out on the verandah."

As I followed her out of the hospital room, I was expecting a medical report on the patient. Imagine my surprise, therefore, when alone on the verandah, Dr. Galena turned to me and said, "Can you help me get a Bible?" I tried not to let my reaction show and asked, "You mean a Bible in Russian?"

She answered in the affirmative and went on to explain. "You see, I found this bookstore here in Conakry that sold Russian Bibles and I bought one. But while I was on vacation in Russia, a friend of mine who had no Bible begged me for it, so I let her keep it. I thought that when I got back to Conakry, I could buy another one. But the store must have moved and I don't know where to find another Bible. Can you help me?"

I said "Of course" and went on to explain that she must have bought her Bible at our Alliance bookstore. Unfortunately, the bookstore had to move and we still hadn't found a suitable place for it. But I told her I was sure there were still Russian Bibles in stock and promised to get one for her.

When I arrived home, I telephoned the church where the bookstore stock was being kept and asked the pastor to put aside a Russian Bible for me. He replied, "But they're all gone. I sold the last one a couple of days ago." I said "Oh no, what will I do now? I've already promised this doctor that I'd get one for her." "You'd better start praying!" was the pastor's helpful advice.

A few days later, the pastor called me to say that he had picked up a package at the post office for the Mission. I said I would get it that evening after prayer meeting. When I got home, I put the small package on the chair. Just books, I thought, and I can open it tomorrow. Suddenly it dawned on me! The package was from the Slavic Gospel Mission, an organization that had from time to time been sending Gospel literature in Russian, to help evangelize the Russian expatriate community in Guinea. I immediately opened the package and there, with other Russian booklets, were two Bibles!

Dr. Galena got her Bible, along with other Gospel booklets, a gift in answer to prayer from people who were concerned. My wife and I delivered the Bible to her in person at her apartment.

I never saw Dr. Galena again. But she and many other Russians who live overseas, have found that it is possible to get Bibles and carry them secretly back to Russia. And we have God's promise that His Word "will not return void." We believe that He will bring salvation and life to those who are searching for the truth.

MIS-SPEAK

MISSIONARIES USUALLY HAVE to learn one or two languages, sometimes more. The language-learning process can often be intimidating and sometimes funny. Missionaries going to French-speaking countries in Africa, have gone to France for this initiation. In 1954, while we were at the Villa Emmanuel in France, we began this process. And we were regaled by the stories of previous students who had been at this facility. One of these colleagues took his suit to the local dry cleaners, and the lady behind the counter asked him, "Etes-vous pressé?" (Are you in a hurry, that is, to get your suit done quickly?) And he replied, "Oui, oui, nettoyé et pressé." He thought he was saying "Yes, cleaned and pressed!" That was Joe Ost. Will Rogers once said, "Everything is funny as long as it happens to someone else."

I was born in Guinea, West Africa and grew up bi-lingually. I was 15 when I left Africa, and 30 when I returned with Florine. I could still read from the Maninka New Testament and understood a lot of what I was hearing. But I could say very little in Maninka; everything came out in French. It took about one month, and speaking Maninka all came back to me. Each day I was amazed at the words that I was able to use. This gift probably made me over-confident, and that was when my mis-speak episode happened.

One day I drove my pickup truck to the Niger River to get some sand for cement work, and I brought two fellows along to shovel it in. A tall young woman walked by and said in a cheerful voice, "Tibabu kye, I ni wali." (White man, hello), a usual greeting. Thinking quickly that she looked young enough to be unmarried, and was larger than just a girl, I tried to match her greeting with "Sungudun ba, I ni wali." I thought I was saying "Big, unmarried woman, hello." She got so mad, she started cursing, and as she left in a huff, she hurled back at me, "These white people, their women don't even braid their hair!"

I was left with my mouth open. The guys were leaning on their shovels and trying to suppress their laughter. "What did I say?" I asked them, but they wouldn't say a word. I kept thinking, "How can this be?" The word "ba" in Maninka means big, great, important. You can say "a big or important person, a big or important man or woman, or a big or husky young man." So, what's wrong with a big, strong young woman?

When I got back to the house, I asked someone else what "sungudun ba" (a big, young woman) was. He said, "Oh, Mister Paul, that's a loose woman, a prostitute." I was floored! And to think that I didn't know that woman and could never apologize to her for such a shameful remark.

Years later I was getting ready to leave the mission station for a trip to our MK school. Millie, one of the missionary women at the Bible School, brought a letter for me to take to her three girls at school. I took one look at the envelope and handed it back to her. "No way," I said. "I'm not delivering a letter addressed like that." "Why not?" she said, "What's the matter with it?" I said, "Look who it's addressed to: The Loose Girls." Their family name was Loose, but I just couldn't do that!

Lesson learned! Ah, the nuances of language. All languages have them. Some mis-speaks are funny, others are not so funny and may have unintended and lingering consequences. For me, that was over 60 years ago and, as you can see, I still remember it well. The Psalmist, David, in Psalm 141:3 (TEV) wrote, "Lord, place a guard at my mouth, a sentry at the door of my lips."

AIRPORT FIASCO

WHEN OUR CHILDREN reached high school, we had to send them to Ivory Coast Academy (ICA). David and Keith finished high school in the U.S., while Sandie and Karyn attended and graduated from ICA. And we drove the long distance from Guinea to Ivory Coast to attend their graduation exercises.

Getting our children to and from ICA was worrisome from a parent's standpoint. We had to say "goodbye," put them on a plane, and trust that they would be able to get to where they were supposed to go, all on their own. For the older ones, that seemed to work well, but the younger ones needed some supervision. We always arranged for one of our missionaries to meet them at the airport and take them to their accommodations for the night or take them to whoever was driving them to the school. There was no way to communicate and stay in touch with them during the trip, and for us that was scary.

One time, Karyn was coming home for Christmas vacation, and we went out to the airport in Conakry to welcome her. The plane arrived and taxied over to the terminal where we were watching from the outside balcony. We watched the passengers come down the steps off the plane, including three or four American kids. We also saw Karyn's white suitcase off-loaded, put on a cart and brought into the terminal. But no Karyn! Finally, one of the American girls looked up at us on the balcony and asked if we were Karyn's parents. We said that we were and she told us that Karyn was on the plane, but got off because Steve Gardner was having a problem, and they wouldn't let him on the plane.

So, that was it. At least we knew a bit about why she wasn't on the plane. Steve Gardner, son of fellow Alliance workers with us in Guinea, was a younger boy and needed help, so Karyn got off the plane to help him. That was typical of Karyn. But the next flight to come here wasn't for three or four days, so what were they going to do? Who was going to help them and take care of them? Karyn had just turned 16 and Steve was only 13. There was no way to contact them. We just had to entrust them to the Lord and to His care and keeping.

Karyn and Steve were with a group of kids leaving ICA and had been driven from the school in Bouake to the airport in Abidjan, the capital, about a five-hour drive. They checked in and got their boarding passes for their flight, but when they got to customs, Steve realized he didn't have his passport. The two of them had gotten a quick bite to eat at the airport and Steve thought he must have left his passport at the restaurant.

Karyn decided to get on the plane and let the flight attendants know that Steve went back to find his passport and that he was on his way. But they were ready to close the doors and wouldn't wait for Steve. Switching between limited French and English, Karyn tried to explain the problem, but in the end, she had to beg them to let her get off the plane. She just couldn't leave Steve behind to fend for himself!

Well, Steve found his passport, but when he got back to customs, the line was very long.

So here they were, two foreign kids stuck at the airport with no money and no adults to help them out. There was a mission station in Abidjan, but Karyn and Steve didn't know where it was or how to get there. Karyn decided they should try to get a taxi to take them, even though they had no cash. Someone from the airport called a taxi for them. It was dark by this time, and eventually a taxi stopped and picked them up. It took some time to communicate to the taxi driver where they wanted to go. He finally agreed to take them to the mission, and wait for Karyn to get the money for the taxi fare from the missionaries.

When they arrived at the mission, Karyn went to the front door of one of the houses that still had lights on. Joe Ost, a missionary who happened to be a friend of ours, came to the door! He paid the taxi driver, invited Karyn and Steve to stay with him and his wife until they could get the next flight out to Conakry. And that's what happened.

Joe was able to radio the next day to let me know what flight the kids would be on. We were there at Conakry airport to welcome them finally and we thanked the Lord for seeing them through an awful situation. Sometime after this, the Alliance decided that all traveling minor MK students should be accompanied by an adult.

> *For he will command his angels concerning you*
> *to guard you in all your ways.*
> *On their hands they will bear you up, lest you*
> *strike your foot against a stone.*
> *Psalm 91:11-12*

THE EVACUATION

I N 1986 FLORINE began to have jaw pain and then bouts of fever and physical weakness, a prolonged one in March and April. She got markedly better just two days before we were to leave for Rochester, New York, for our daughter Karyn's wedding in June.

We were able to attend Karyn's graduation from nursing school at Roberts Wesleyan College, as well as her wedding. Florine was able to see a neurologist and was diagnosed with trigeminal neuralgia, a facial nerve condition. He prescribed Tegretol to relieve the extreme pain.

After one month in the U.S., we returned to our ministry at the Telekoro Bible Institute. Our daughter, Sandie and husband Steve, came to Africa in July to visit us, and we were able to travel around some with them before they returned to the U.S. Just after their visit, Florine began to have facial pain, bouts of fever and weakness again. Medication didn't seem to help.

There was a mission organization called Mission Philafricaine (the Swiss mission), who had opened a medical work in Macenta. Through radio communication with them, their doctor, Dr. Hannes Wiher, prescribed Ampicillin for Florine. We were able to buy it in our local market. When that treatment had no effect, the doctor asked us to come down to their facility in Macenta, where he would be better able to treat Florine. We only packed clothes for three days, hoping the doctor would be able to iron out her problem.

After ten days in Macenta, and with her temperature hovering between 104–106 degrees, the doctor said Florine would have to be evacuated to Europe as soon as possible. She had uncontrolled septicemia with severe urinary infection, damaged liver and kidneys, etc. The doctor was trying to get Florine out on Sunday, the next day! He thought the 20-hour road trip to Conakry would possibly kill her, and there were no planes available to come to this forest location of Macenta until Monday.

Dr. Wiher felt that Florine was too weak to go to the U.S. or Europe by a regular airline flight. Through the help of the Swiss mission, a Lear Jet of the Swiss Air Rescue service would come to Conakry on Monday to take her to Switzerland. The doctor also arranged for a special flight by Air Guinea to come to Macenta early Monday morning to take us to Conakry.

Early Monday morning at the Macenta airport, we were just in time for the last call from the Air Guinea special flight before it turned around and went back empty to Conakry. Florine was lifted into the plane on a blanket and laid on three seat cushions placed on the floor of the plane. The Swiss nurse accompanied us to Conakry. We arrived in Conakry before the Swiss Air Rescue jet got there, so we stayed at a local motel. Our Guinean colleague, Pastor Isaac Keita, was there to wave a blanket over Florine to make a little air movement for her.

When the Swiss jet arrived, we were taken to the airport. The plane crew came over to get Florine and prepare her for the flight. But they told me that they didn't have room for me on the plane. I would have to go to Switzerland by commercial flight. When Florine heard that, she told them that if I didn't go on the plane with her, she wouldn't go either! While the crew discussed this, Pastor Isaac and other Christians prayed with us and entreated Florine to go on this flight for her critical health situation. The flight crew decided they would make room for me on the plane, but that I would have to move around to accommodate the needs of the crew. Since it was a long flight, the pilots would need to have room to sleep.

Aboard the small jet plane, the main space was taken up by the bunk that Florine was put on, and she was connected to a number of medical devices and monitors with a nurse right there to keep track of everything. What I noticed from where I sat was her temperature . . . fixed at 106 degrees!

Over the Sahara Desert the captain received instructions for the plane to take us to Geneva instead of Zurich, Switzerland. When we arrived in Geneva, we were met by an ambulance, which drove us 60 kilometers to the city of Lausanne, where Florine was admitted to the University Hospital of the Canton of Vaud. The doctor who had arranged for our plane to come to Geneva was there. We knew him from the Swiss mission in Macenta and because he knew of Florine's condition, was able to arrange it for us.

Florine was in intensive care isolation for over three days, where they kept her condition stable, while looking for the tropical "microbe" which they suspected might have caused her condition. Dr. Wiher in Macenta had labeled the cause of her illness as an allergic reaction to the medication Tegretol and had taken her off it before we left Africa. In Switzerland they never found the "microbe" they suspected. Florine's temperature, which remained high with spurts to 106, began to drop and finally stayed normal. The doctors couldn't explain that. They determined that the "microbe" was no longer active. But we knew that people on three continents were praying, and we believed that the Lord had answered prayer. We praise Him for providing for us through a most difficult time.

After 18 days in the hospital, Florine was released, and we were invited to stay in a lovely guest room with the De Benoit sisters, who worked for the Swiss mission. They were so welcoming and generous, and we appreciated their kind hospitality. Florine was feeling much better, but her physical strength came back very slowly. In the meantime, Florine's doctor put her back on Tegretol; she just wouldn't believe what Dr. Wiher had written about Florine being allergic to this medication.

On November 12, 1986, we returned to our work in Guinea after 86 days of treatment and recuperation in Switzerland. While our medical insurance only covered a small part of the evacuation costs,

The Christian & Missionary Alliance picked up the remaining tab, for which we are forever grateful.

It is amazing to look back now and recognize God's miraculous providence in this whole situation, even in the small details. To God be the glory!

Florine enjoying her recuperation

81

EVACUATED AGAIN!

WE ARRIVED BACK at the Telekoro Bible Institute in mid-November 1986. Christmas was always a big celebration at the school. The rice harvest was usually finished and the students' school debts paid off by graduation time in January. The new school year didn't begin until the month of May, so we had some time to relax a bit.

Our son, David and his wife, Heidi came to Guinea in April to introduce us to our first grandchild, Kristen Marie, born in September. They arrived at Telekoro just in time to accompany us on our monthly trip to Macenta for Florine's health checkup at the Swiss mission.

They found that Florine's septicemia had returned, and Dr. Wiher wanted to evacuate her to the U.S. this time, while she was able to make it on a regular airline flight. He stopped the Tegretol she was taking, and sent us back to Telekoro. He arrived the next day to prepare Florine for the long trip to the capital, Conakry, and on to the U.S. He was accompanied by a nurse, Elisabeth, who apparently had the same type O negative blood as Florine. In our daughter's bedroom, Florine in one bed and Elisabeth in the other, the doctor performed a direct blood transfusion. This new blood perked Florine up for the long trip to Conakry the next day.

In Conakry, everything went unusually well in preparation for our departure the next evening. The blood transfusion had really helped Florine to perk up. On our plane to Brussels, Florine was on a stretcher lying across the backs of six seats in the rear of the plane. My seat was one of three extra seats beside Florine's stretcher, and the captain allowed David and Heidi to take the other two empty seats and hold the baby on their lap.

We arrived in Brussels on Sunday morning – Easter Sunday! There were more seats available on the flight from Brussels to New York, so we could spread out a little more. We could hear baby Kristen cooing or crying from where we sat. Our son, Keith and daughter-in-law, Krista met the plane in New York and we were able to visit with them before our flight to Rochester, where we stayed with Karyn.

At the hospital in Rochester, we learned that a surgeon in Pittsburgh had recently developed a surgery that corrects trigeminal neuralgia. Up until then, the only surgery available was to sever the nerve that was causing the pain. We received a phone call from Fran Bozeman, a missionary who served in Irian Jaya, Indonesia, and she had the same condition as Florine. Her surgeon had initially cut the nerve, but the nerve eventually grew back together, so all her pain returned. She came back to the U.S. and consulted with another surgeon, who had just seen a report about a new surgery to repair trigeminal neuralgia. A surgeon at Duke University in Durham, North Carolina was performing this surgery. Fran had just recovered from that surgery when she heard about Florine and called us. "I'm free, I'm free!" I remember her saying on the phone, "The pain is gone!" And now she was getting ready to head back to Indonesia.

It turned out that Fran's surgeon had been an assistant surgeon working with Dr. Peter Jannetta at Pittsburgh General Hospital. Dr. Janetta was the one who had pioneered this new surgery, and Florine's neurologist in Rochester referred her to Dr. Janetta.

The surgery is a delicate operation. An incision is made behind the right ear, and a small cushion inserted between the blood vessel and the nerve, which has lost some of its natural insulation. That seems simple. But officially it's called "micro-vascular decompression of the fifth cranial nerve."

While awaiting Florine's scheduled surgery in Pittsburgh, we were able to drive to Nyack, New York, and attend our son Keith's seminary graduation from Nyack College. That was an unexpected blessing! Florine was on strong medication in order to be able to be there.

Her surgery was Dr. Jannetta's last operation he performed before leaving the U.S. for an extended tour in Europe. He stopped in to see Florine in recovery and asked about her pain. "It's all gone!" she was able to tell him.

Following a short convalescence, we were able to return to Guinea in June to complete our last term of missionary service at the Telekoro Bible Institute. We were able to finish strong, which only a year and a half earlier had seemed impossible due to Florine's medical condition!

When we returned to the U.S. in 1989, we made a stop-over in Switzerland to see our friends who had been so kind to us in our time of need, and show them what God had done. We also stopped in at the hospital to see the doctor who had been in charge of Florine's recuperation in 1986. We told her about the new surgical procedure that had brought healing to the trigeminal neuralgia, hoping that she would be able to help others with this condition.

Because of the newness of Florine's surgical procedure for trigeminal neuralgia, she had to write an annual report for Dr. Jannetta for a few years. He wanted to track her progress following the surgery.

Twenty-three years after her surgery, and retirement to Florida, Florine's facial pain began to return. We called Dr. Jannetta in Pittsburgh, and he offered to re-do the surgery. Apparently, the nerve had elongated with age and was contacting the blood vessel beyond the little "cushion" that had been installed, creating that familiar trigeminal pain. But Dr. Jannnetta also told Florine that there were newer and better medications available now, which he recommended. And so, for the last ten years a new medication has kept Florine pain free.

God has been so good to us. To Him be the glory.

CAPTURING THE MOMENT

T HE C&MA MISSIONARIES had an annual conference at Kankan, in Guinea. Missionaries came from Sudan (now Mali), Upper Volta (now Burkina Faso), Ivory Coast (now Côte d'Ivoire) and Guinea, for this large gathering. But after Guinea gained its independence in 1958, it was just the Guinea field missionaries who gathered for the annual get-together.

In 1964, at one such annual conference in Kankan, Dr. Nathan Bailey, then president of The Christian & Missionary Alliance, was the speaker at the conference. On the Monday after the close of the conference, the missionaries from Mamou and Conakry took the train from Kankan, to return to their stations of ministry. Our Guinean cook returned from the market that morning and reported that the train had had an accident upon leaving the station and that some of the passengers had been injured. The missionaries still remaining at the conference jumped into their vehicles and headed off to the train. I was the last one to leave, just as Dr. Bailey showed up and asked if he could ride along.

There was a crowd of people milling around, as we arrived at the scene. The train coaches were still upright, but off the tracks, probably from a switch malfunction. All of our missionaries on the train were okay. I immediately went looking for any injured passengers, to see if they needed a ride to the hospital. We had heard there was a man who had broken his arm, but he and the other injured people had been taken care of.

Then I heard Dr. Bailey calling me, so I hurried over to him. "Paul, please tell me what this man is trying to tell me," he said. I turned to the man and he introduced himself to me in French. He was an inspector for the railroad and said that this foreign man was taking unauthorized photos and that he had to confiscate his camera. I translated that for Dr. Bailey who said "Tell him that I can't give him my camera." The railroad inspector responded, "I have the authority to seize his camera."

During the time period when Guinea adopted a socialist-style government, taking pictures was outlawed. The socialist leaders wanted to control all public relations and having pictures taken by a U.S. pastor could have damaged the career of the railroad inspector.

Just then, we saw our mission chairman, Mike Kurlak, who was nearby, speaking with the Kankan police chief. Dr. Bailey thought he might be the one to intercede with the railroad inspector for him. I spoke in French to Mike, relating to him the problem and he, in proper African Fashion, consulted the police chief concerning the problem. The police chief proceeded to berate the inspector for treating a foreigner this way for such a minor thing. The inspector calmly informed the chief that he was the one who had the authority in this matter, not the chief, and that his seizing the camera was necessary. Of course, I was translating this into English for Dr. Bailey.

Dr. Bailey expressed to the chief that most of the pictures taken on his camera were taken in countries other than Guinea, and he really couldn't afford to lose them. He promised that when he returned to the States and had the film developed, he would destroy the train wreck photos.

The railroad inspector wouldn't agree to that, but Dr. Bailey had another idea. Would there be a photographer available with a dark room who could open the camera, cut off the pictures of the train wreck and develop them, to the satisfaction of the inspector? Well, there happened to be a photographer whose shop was right across the street from our mission compound in Kankan. The police chief had to do some talking, but the railroad inspector finally agreed. We all drove to the little shop and into the small dark room crowded the photographer, the railroad inspector, Dr. Bailey, the police chief, and Mike Kurlak.

The photographer cut off the last part of the film, developed it to see the photos. The inspector said, "There are more." So the photographer went through the process again, cutting off another piece of the film. The inspector still wasn't satisfied that all the train wreck photos had been cut off, so again another piece of the film was clipped off. Finally, the inspector was satisfied that all the wreck photos had been dealt with. The men came out of the dark room smiling, shook hands and departed.

But that's not quite the end of the story. That summer, our family returned to the U.S. for furlough. I was on my fall missions tour and speaking at a church in Toronto, Canada. I bumped into Dr. Nathan Bailey. He said, "Paul, do you remember the problem with those photos of the train wreck in Kankan and how the photographer took them off the film for me? Well, when I got home and had my film developed, I found I still had three pictures of the train wreck, and I'm not destroying them either!"

GOD SPEAKS MY LANGUAGE

THE NUMBER OF missionaries on the field had been depleted during the war time, but with the end of WW2, new missionaries came to the field beginning in the late 1940s. Arnold and Anna Mae Ratzloff were new missionaries assigned to work among the Toma people in the Macenta area of Guinea.

The ministry in Macenta was being carried out by Cova, the evangelist who was instrumental in taking the gospel to his people, the Tomas. Now, with many converts in that area, the Ratzloffs felt the necessity of translating the New Testament into the Toma language. In addition to their main ministry of taking the gospel to the outer villages, the new missionary couple also took the burden of translation upon themselves with zeal. They spent many years in Macenta, working on translation.

In 1967 all foreign church workers, both Catholic and Protestant, were asked to leave the country. The government felt that the church should be run by its own people, the Guineans, so the missionaries would not be needed. But the aim of our mission was to "ready" the nationals and when enough men went through the training to become pastors and church leaders, they would be able to take over the ministry. An exception was finally made, and those at the Telekoro Bible Institute, and the Mamou Alliance Academy, were permitted to remain in Guinea. Florine and I were privileged to be able to stay.

Arnold and Anna Mae Ratzloff happened to be on furlough in the U.S. during the 1967 crisis. When our chairman in the capital had to be replaced, Arnold Ratzloff was to be the new chairman. We applied for a visa to get the Ratzloffs back into Guinea, but the visa was denied a number of times. I made monthly trips from the Bible Institute to the capital to try to get their visa approved. The head of Security finally told me that he couldn't help me. When I asked what else I could do, he offered to introduce me to the government minister. He took me to the minister's office where I met his assistant. The assistant told me that the country was only accepting 15% of all visa requests, but since the government had nothing against us as a Mission, if we really needed this visa approval, he would see what he could do for me.

Two days later I had the visa for the Ratzloffs. Florine and I, with the two other missionaries from the Conakry office, went to a restaurant to celebrate. While we were at the restaurant, the United States ambassador saw us there and came over to ask us what we were celebrating. "The visa approval for the Ratzloffs," I replied. He couldn't believe me. I had asked for his help before in securing the visa, and he had told me that he couldn't help me. He then asked, "The visa was granted on your request?" I replied, "It was my request, but it was the Lord that got the minister to approve it."

The Ratzloffs had a good ministry in Conakry. They were able to get the translation for the Toma New Testament to the Bible Society for printing. But Arnold developed a health problem, later diagnosed as miasthenia gravis, and finally had to be evacuated to the U.S. for treatment. The Ratzloffs had been looking forward to the arrival of the printed Toma New Testaments and being able to take them to Macenta and present them to the Toma Church. Now they wouldn't be able to do this. They made me promise that I would do it for them, and I felt privileged to do this.

The Toma New Testaments finally arrived in Conakry and I tried to make arrangements as soon as possible to take them to Macenta for the presentation. It was toward the end of the rainy season, and the last part of the road to Macenta was not paved. The Swiss mission in Guinea, Mission Philafricaine, had its main station at Macenta, and some of their personnel happened to be traveling to Macenta with a

Jeep and a large truck. They invited me to go along with them. On the last unpaved stretch, the road got pretty muddy, and the Jeep got bogged down in the mud. Fortunately, the truck traveling with us was able to pull us out.

The Toma Christians were so happy to have their New Testament, and my presentation that Sunday morning was a real blessing. I met one of the church elders, Akoi, who was a tailor by profession. I took a picture of Akoi holding his New Testament to his heart. As I snapped his picture he was saying, "God speaks my language!"

Akoi holding his new Ioma New Testament

A ROYAL PYTHON

IN AFRICA WHEN you are driving at night, you often come across large snakes warming themselves on the sunbaked roads. These are often poisonous vipers. I usually tried to protect some night-time local walkers by stopping my vehicle, using my .22 rifle to dispatch the snake and throw it off the road. Or I might have used my machete to chop off the head and leave the rest on the road for some traveler. Viper meat is really good!

My Aunt Grace Patterson was a long-time missionary at Kankan. Early on she taught at the girls' school in Baro, and was involved in other women's ministries and translation work. I was moving her to the Telekoro Bible School, and it was dark before we left Kankan. Along the way we came across a large snake warming itself in the middle of the road. I stopped the car back far enough to keep the snake in the headlight. I got my rifle and was about to shoot the snake in the head when I realized that this snake was no viper. It was a royal python, a non-venomous snake more that five feet long with a girth about the size of my arm. It is called a ball python, because when disturbed, it rolls itself into a ball. I had been thinking for some time about getting one of these to keep as a pet - an unusual pet to be sure - but harmless. And here was one all ready for the taking, except that I wasn't quite sure about picking it up, because I had never done that before. I hesitated, trying to be sure that this was something I could really do. The snake must have decided that he was in danger as he began to move slowly toward the brush at the edge of the road. I tried to stop it by setting my rifle butt down on its back, but this only made it move faster. I realized that the only way to keep this snake from getting away was to grab it with my hand. A quick decision, and it rolled into a ball, much to my relief.

Back at the car, my aunt was fuming about the insanity of picking up a wild snake. "Paul," she was saying, "You're crazy! We are miles from any hospital, there's no doctor anywhere near, and I don't even have a band-aid!" I tried to reassure her, "Look, it's rolled into a ball. It is really a ball python and not at all dangerous." She answered, "So what are you going to do with it?" And I said, "I'm going to take it home with us." Well, the only thing I had in the car was an old cloth double-panel baby diaper that I used as a rag. I cut the end off, which made a bag to put the snake in, and I asked my aunt to tie the string while I held it. All the way home she kept asking me if the bag and the snake were still behind my feet.

My kids were more interested in a pet royal python than my Aunt Grace was. And at the Bible School, I had plenty of students who could get field mice for food for our new pet. We named him Oscar. Our son David, especially took to Oscar and was a big help in taking care of him. Two years later, we were headed to the U.S. for furlough and decided to take Oscar with us. I went to some effort and expense to get a Certificate of Origin and a Certificate of Health from the Forestry Department in Kissidougou, hoping this would avoid any problem getting a snake through customs and into the U.S.

Our trip to the U.S. included a 3-day side trip to London. We had to spend the night in Paris, and we didn't want to take Oscar to London with us. We knew some former missionaries from Viet Nam, a pastor and his wife, who lived in Paris, and they agreed to keep Oscar while we were in London. David and Keith went with me on the Paris subway to take Oscar. He was in a box that I had made for the trip, and I told them all they would have to do was keep him in the box – no feeding, no water, just keep him in the box. When we returned to Paris, we went to pick up Oscar and found that the pastor's wife had had a youth group meeting at their house while we were gone. She had taken Oscar out of the box and had enjoyed handling him and showing him to the young people. They were impressed!

When we got to New York, we put Oscar in a cloth bag, which David carried. At Customs, when asked if we had anything to declare, I said, "We have a live python to declare, sir." The officer said, "Take it over to the Health Department." At that desk we found the officer busy writing and without looking up, he said, "Yes?" And I said, "We have a live python to declare, sir." Well, that brought his head up, and he asked, "Where is it?" "Here in this bag. Do you want to see it?" He was already pushing his chair away from the desk. "No," he said. "Well, I have these special papers for it. Don't you need to see them?" "No," was his reply. "But don't you have to sign them?" "No, not unless you insist." "I'd like you to sign them." So, he reluctantly signed my papers. "What do I do now?" I asked. "Take it and go," was his answer. And I think he was glad to get rid of us.

Oscar was an interesting and unusual pet. One thing we had to do when we got settled in Jamestown, New York, was to find a way to feed him. I went to the pet store there and asked how much large mice cost. The lady asked, "What do you want to do with them?" This was the question I was hoping to avoid. But I answered honestly, "Feed them to my snake." "Oh," she said, "we have some other customers who get mice here for their pet snakes." That made me feel better.

I couldn't take Oscar with me on my Missions tours, but once when my tour took me to Erie, Pennsylvania, just 50 miles from Jamestown, I invited Florine to come for the Missions Dinner and bring Oscar along. We put his box in a Sunday School room and announced that those who might be interested in seeing a live royal python from Africa could see it there. Of course, a lot of the younger folks went to see him. Oscar was a big hit. Quite a few years later, I was back at that same church in Erie, as a missionary speaker. After the service, a woman with a small boy came up to me, handed me a photo and asked if I remembered it. It was of a younger girl sporting a royal python around her neck!

David also had his fun with Oscar. He was invited once to speak to a youth group at a church near where he was living in Frewsburg, New York. He took Oscar with him in a cloth bag, and put the bag on the front pew beside him. When the singing was over, the pianist came and sat down beside David. When he got up to speak and pulled the python out of the bag, she jumped up, ran down the aisle and out the door, and kept on going!

Oscar stayed with David in the U.S. when we returned to Guinea the next year. When he finished high school and prepared to go away to Houghton College, he wondered what he was going to do with Oscar. But before he went to college, Oscar died, which took care of the problem, but left a lot of great memories.

A few years later, Oscar was to be replaced by another pet royal python. Karyn, the youngest of our four children, was attending middle school in Kabala, Sierra Leone. She came home for Christmas and her present for me was a royal python. She had purchased him from a young man there at Kabala. We named him Samba, a typical African name.

After Karyn graduated from High School, she brought Samba to the U.S. He lived with Karyn in Rochester, New York, New Haven, Connecticut, and up until 2020, has been in Orlando, Florida, where she kept him in a clear plastic-paneled cage in the corner of her living room. She has fed Samba mice and rats, cleaned his cage, filled his bowl with water, and has, with her children, played with him to give him exercise and attention. Karyn got married in 2020 and moved to Melbourne, Florida. That's where Samba lives now. 40 years, as of this writing, and Samba is still part of the family!

David with Oscar

96

THE THIEF'S REWARD

SOME TIME AFTER Guinea had gained its independence, the political environment changed from colonialism to socialism. Public execution became a means to punish wrong doing for crimes that we would not consider capital offenses. By making the executions public, the new regime felt there would be better obeyance to all of the laws.

Florine needed a loaf of French bread for supper, and I offered to drive to the market in town to get it. Keith wanted to go along for the ride. As we got into town, we noticed an unusual number of people milling about. And then Keith saw it – a man was hanging from a tree limb by a rope around his neck.

"Look, Dad," he said. While I understood why the man had been hanged in public, and had witnessed several other public executions, I didn't know how to explain the harsh nature of the punishment to my son. We were both overwhelmed and Keith said, "Dad, forget the bread, let's go home." Which we did.

Another time I was in town and stopped at the police station for something. What couldn't be missed was the human arm, suspended by a rope and swaying in the breeze over the entrance to the office. The police chief told me that this young man had stolen more than a hundred head of cattle and had finally been caught. The local authorities wanted to have a public execution of the fellow on an up-coming holiday. For this they needed authorization from the capital, which didn't come in time. So, they handed out the typical Muslim punishment for a thief – they cut off his arm. And to make it a lesson for possible future thieves, they suspended the arm in plain view over the entrance to the police station. The chief told me that the thief was in the hospital recuperating.

When I returned to the Bible Institute campus, my Aunt Grace Patterson, a teacher at the school, was really taken by the story about this thief who had lost his arm. She insisted that I contact the police chief for permission for her to visit this young man and read God's Word to him in his language. The chief's response was, "Please do, he needs it!"

Aunt Grace visited the young man, who was from the Fula tribe. She read to him from the New Testament in the Fula language. She returned with an enthusiastic report. "He seems to be such a nice young man and is interested in God's Word." She wanted me to set up another visit for her.

Not too long after this, I ran into the chief of police in town. He told me, "Remember that young Fula man that was in the hospital because we took his arm off for stealing cattle, and your Aunt visited and read the Bible to him? Well, he stole the money from the fellow in the bed next to him at the hospital, and has disappeared! We have no idea where he is."

We never found out what happened to the young man Aunt Grace reached out to with the Gospel. I hope that, like the thief on the cross beside Jesus, the young man repented and sought the Lord's grace prior to losing another arm or worse.

HALLOWEEN PRANK

IT WAS MY sophomore year at Houghton College, and I was a WW2 veteran with a car. Most students didn't have vehicles in the '40s. A group of "friends" had decided to liven things up a bit on Halloween evening, by pulling a mock raid on the college library. The plan was to haul off the bust of William Shakespeare, but they needed an escape vehicle. That's how I came to be involved. I was a little older than they were and I realized that the bust was made of plaster, which could be easily damaged, and which would get us in real trouble. When I refused to be involved in that, the guys decided to take the big silver Loving Cup, instead. It was unbreakable, and they would deposit it in another administrative building.

The night came and two guys pushed noisily into the quiet library with their faces masked, carrying cap pistols, and announcing, "This is a stick-up!" When a student at a nearby table stood up to protest, one of the guys fired a couple of shots at the protester, who was actually in on the deal. He brought his hand up to his white shirt, smearing it with ketchup and cried out, "I've been shot!" The other intruder hastened over to the desk to prevent the librarian from using the phone to call for help. The two then grabbed the Loving Cup, ran down the stairs, out the door, and jumped into my waiting car. I drove away without turning on my headlights so that any possible witness would not be able to get my license number.

We thought that everything went as planned. After all, it was just a prank! But the school dean happened to be nearby, and although he couldn't read my license plate, he recognized my car. So the next day, we learned that Dr. Bob had it pretty much figured out, and what we thought was a harmless prank turned out to be a one-week suspension from school, for each of us. And we had to leave the campus for that week. Dr. Bob suggested that we could work out on the college farm, which I declined! And I learned that another friend, Bill, was also suspended for a week for being involved in another prank. He was caught whitewashing the celebrated large rock at the campus entrance, the symbol of Houghton College being "founded on the Rock".

I chose to drive the 300 some miles back to Flint, Michigan, where I lived with my Grandmother Patterson when not in school. When she asked why I wasn't at school, I told her that I was caught up with my studies and needed a little break . . . what I considered at the time an acceptable "white lie." Bill also returned to Detroit, and we agreed to both grow a mustache and to meet in Detroit on Saturday, so we could attend the Youth for Christ meeting together. When I arrived and found Bill, he was a bit upset because his mustache wasn't all that visible – Bill had blond hair. I found an old cork in my car, and burnt it with a match and applied some black to Bill's blond mustache. We had a great time at the YFC meeting, fake mustache and all!

Back at Houghton after our week of suspension, we tried to apply ourselves to our studies. I did receive a poor semester grade in Greek because of that escapade. So, was that it? No, not quite.

Twenty years later, our oldest son, David, was a student at Houghton and was invited to a friend's wedding. The wedding was in Indiana, at a church where the father of the bride-to-be was the pastor. When he met David, the pastor asked him if he was related to Paul Ellenberger, and David said, "He's my dad." The pastor asked him if his father had told him about the Halloween incident and getting kicked out of Houghton for a week, to which David had to say, "No."

Well, that pastor was my friend, Bill, who filled David in on "the Halloween prank." So much for your kids thinking you never got into trouble.

A POCKET DAY BOOK

I T WAS A Sunday morning, and I had driven to a village where I was the invited preacher. Typically, the message would be interpreted in the local dialect, which means the sermon would take twice as long. But then, that's not a problem in Africa. At some conferences where several language groups may be present, it's not unusual to have two, three, or even four interpreters, which make a sermon even longer. But people often walk to church from outlying villages, so they come for the service, no matter how long it takes.

I decided that before the meeting began, I should use the bathroom. Well, in the village things are a bit different. The "bathroom" was a hole in the ground out in the yard, surrounded by a 7-foot-tall fence of plaited reeds, with a common entrance. My concern was not privacy, but my pocket day book, which I always carried in my upper jacket pocket. This little book not only had a record of dates and times, but also other important information. As head of the mission station and the Bible Institute, I was responsible for expenses, transactions and other business records, which were often sizeable. I kept all this information in the little book until the end of the month, when I wrote up my regular financial statement.

In the facility, I carefully took off my jacket that had the day book in the upper jacket pocket, used the facility, and got the jacket to put back on. I tried to be so careful, but for some reason, as I was getting my other arm in, that little book popped out of the pocket, flipped up in the air, and dropped down in the hole. I was just flabbergasted! This can't be! The sun was up high enough to let me see down the hole. And there was my little book, not in the bottom as I expected, but caught on a small ledge in the side of the hole wall and about three or four feet from the bottom. Lord, help us, as my dad used to say in times of danger or stress.

I left the enclosure, found a local fellow who seemed old enough to care, and showed him my problem. I asked him if he could find a long bamboo pole, an African hoe and some bark rope for me. He returned quickly with the items, tied the hoe tightly to the end of the bamboo pole, and started to go after my little book. I stopped him saying that if he didn't succeed, I would have him to blame for it, but if I bungled the job, I would only have myself to blame.

Carefully, and certainly with the Lord's help, I lowered the long bamboo pole with the hoe edge to where the little book was, slid the blade of the hoe under the book, and slowly, painstakingly, lifted the bamboo pole up until my helper was able to grab the little book.

Praise the Lord for His help in a bad situation. And I wasn't even late for church!

A RISKY LANDING

OUR DAUGHTER, SANDIE, had graduated from high school at Ivory Coast Academy and was looking forward to going to the States to begin college. She was planning to go to Houghton College in Houghton, New York. Florine and I met at Houghton College in 1947, but I'll save that story for another chapter!

Sending your kids off to school is a big deal for missionaries. I was six when I went to Mamou Alliance Academy in Mamou, Guinea. All four of our children attended Mamou before it closed in 1970. It was hard sending them off to school in Guinea where we lived, and to schools in Sierra Leone and Ivory Coast, neighboring countries. But leaving them in the States to finish high school and go to college as we did with David and Keith was a different story. And putting Sandie on a plane by herself to go to the States for college seemed harder yet.

It was August, the height of the rainy season in Conakry, Guinea. There was always so much rain and stormy weather this time of year. Incoming flights usually made no effort to land in Conakry when the weather was bad, so we were concerned about Sandie's flight. She was booked on Sabena, a Belgian airline, and the flight was to make stops at Monrovia, Liberia, and Dakar, Senegal, before going on to New York. In Dakar, two missionary ladies that we knew, would join her flight. So we prayed, along with colleagues, family and friends in many places for Sandie's departure.

It rained heavily the night before she was to leave, and we awoke to a very foggy morning. It didn't look at all encouraging, and we went

103

to the Conakry airport with a certain apprehension, yet waiting to see how God was going to work it out.

There were three flights due into the airport that morning. The first one was a cargo plane that flew over without making any attempt to land. The second, a passenger plane, also flew over and kept on going. Then in preparation for the third one, Sandie's flight, the workers pushed out the cart loaded with the luggage for the prospective passengers. As the plane's arrival time neared, the passengers and their families also pushed out to the runway (they do things differently in Africa!) to await the plane's arrival.

I happened to be standing next to an American pilot who I knew. He flew for a small plane service based out of Conakry. When the siren went off, announcing the arrival of the plane, and the roar of the passenger jet's engines followed, the plane emerged from the fog. I remember asking my pilot friend, "Is he going to land?" He said, "No, he's too high to land." And the plane went roaring off. That was it! The workers pushed the luggage cart back into the terminal and all the people followed. Obviously that plane was not going to land!

What we were afraid of just happened. Sandie was crying. "What am I going to do now?" she said. We were discussing the situation and trying to figure out what we could do but there didn't seem to be any immediate solution. All of a sudden, we heard this roaring sound, like a plane landing. Yes, it was our Sabena plane . . . it had turned around and come back and landed! Praise the Lord! We hurried to get Sandie ready to board. The guys with the baggage cart had to reload the suitcases and get them back out on the tarmac. We thanked the Lord for answered prayer. Sandie's little sister, Karyn, said "This is the first miracle I've ever seen!"

Well, Sandie got off. Later we asked the Sabena agent why the pilot of that plane decided to come back and land, after passing over the first time. . . they never try a second time! He said he had wondered the same thing, so he asked the pilot. The pilot simply said, "On the first pass over, I saw that everything was in order, so I thought I'd come back again and land." I told the agent, "You know, many people on three continents were praying for this flight and this pilot, and that this plane would be able to land here today. So, it was really God who put it in the pilot's mind to come back and land the plane. We praise God for answered prayer!"

Paul and Florine with Sandie, before all the excitement at the airport.

YOU'RE MY BROTHER

I WAS DRIVING MY Aunt Grace to Conakry for her departure to the U.S. She was retiring after many years of ministry in Guinea. We came to one place where the road went down a long hill and then up again, and because that long stretch of road was straight, you could see the whole distance.

On the way down there was a farm tractor pulling a trailer and going a lot slower than we were. I could see that there was no on-coming traffic, so I passed the tractor and continued on my way. But at the top of the hill there was a police check point, and the policeman stopped me and said that he had to arrest me.

"What did I do?" I responded in French. He replied, "You passed on a hill." "I did," I admitted, "but there was no on-coming traffic." "But you are not allowed to pass on a hill," the policeman persisted. "Oh yes, I can. The Driver's Manual says you can," I reminded him. "Oh no it doesn't," he contradicted.

I tried my best to convince him, without success. So, I turned to my Aunt Grace, and switching to Maninka, our African language, I said to her, "My, but this man just wants to make it hard for me." The policeman took a good look at me and said, "You speak Maninka?" I replied, "Of course I speak Maninka. I was born here in Guinea and grew up here. What do you think?" "I think you're my brother," he said. I agreed with him, and after a brief conversation in Maninka, he wished me well and let us go.

After that, every time I bumped into him in the capital city of Conakry, he would whistle me over for a brotherly greeting – in Maninka.

GOD'S LITTLE MIRACLE

IT WAS FEBRUARY 1958, during our first term of missionary service in Guinea. The Mission wanted to build a motel in the block behind the main campus at Kankan. We held our annual conference in Kankan and this motel would help alleviate the housing problem during the conference. Andy Gardner, the Mission builder, had already begun the project when his wife Norma became ill and had to be evacuated to the U.S. for treatment. John Johanson was called to come from Upper Volta to take over the building project. We were stationed at Faranah at the time, but were asked to move to Kankan for two or three months to help.

It was a two-day driving trip for us to move to Kankan. David was four and a half at the time and Florine was three months pregnant with Keith. The long trip in the heat proved to be exhausting for Florine and we were looking forward to spending the next day resting and recuperating.

But Sunday morning came with complications. Florine woke up with what appeared to be contractions and some bleeding. I went to see if Mrs. Kurlak could call The French doctor (yes, they had telephones in Kankan). He wasn't happy about being disturbed on a Sunday morning, but he came to check Florine. He washed his hands, came dripping into the bedroom, and saw David standing there quietly with his hands behind his back. Looking down on the little boy and articulating his accented English, he said sternly, "GET OUT!" Poor David – he fled the scene!

After examining Florine, the doctor told her that everything would be all right – she needed to stay in bed and rest. But he told Mrs. Kurlak that Florine was in the process of miscarrying and would lose the baby before the day was out. But she didn't tell us that the doctor said that. The Kurlaks had been planning to leave shortly for ministry in a village some distance away. And, of course, I thought all was well and encouraged them to go ahead with their plans.

They prayed for Florine and went, reluctantly. When they returned that afternoon, Helen came right over to find that Florine was resting well – and no sign of a miscarriage! Praise the Lord, God had intervened, and Keith was born six months later, God's little miracle to us!

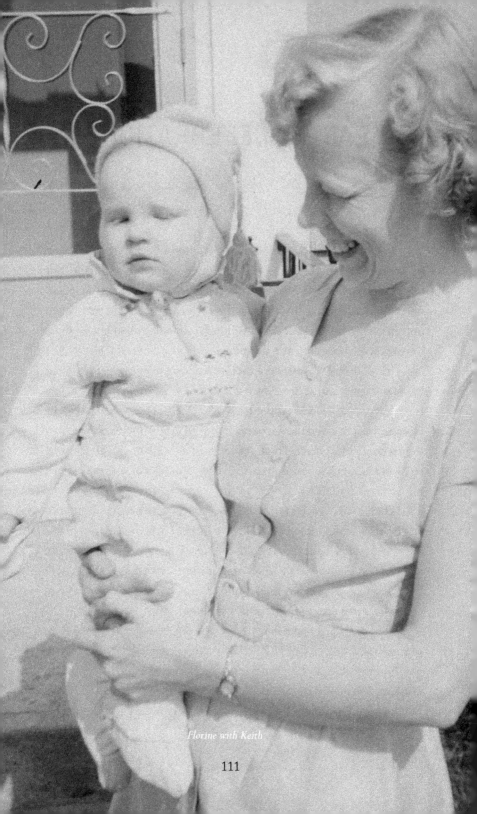

Florine with Keith

EASTER CELEBRATION

AFTER THE 1967 crisis, travel in Guinea became a little more complicated. We had to get a signed authorization from our regional governor every time we needed to leave our region. We could only visit churches by invitation, and we were permitted to participate only in events held in the church building. I should say that I don't think we were ever refused travel permits.

The Church districts were used to having a missionary help them in the ministry, and at first, were desolated by the missionaries' departure. They soon found that the Lord, the Head of the Church, by His Holy Spirit, provided the encouragement and the impetus to proclaim the Gospel with power. The Lord emboldened them to visit new villages and new areas with enthusiasm, and to watch the surge of church growth and maturity.

When I was invited to be the guest speaker at a three-day Easter celebration at the large N'Zérékoré church, I accepted this opportunity gladly. N'Zérékoré was quite a distance from the Bible Institute and missionaries didn't get there to minister very often. But although I was excited about this opportunity, there were signs of some real difficulties that would need to be overcome.

First, we heard that a long bridge was out at some distance before our arrival at the city of N'Zérékoré. Where we lived, there was no gasoline available, and we had no idea when some would be coming to our area. We would need enough gas to make the long trip and return home again. Then there was me – I was sick with the complications of a really bad cold and infection, which had taken away my voice. And I was to be the main speaker!

I prayed a lot over this situation, and the more I prayed the more I felt that God wanted me to go anyway. So even though the list I made of pros and cons was mostly negative, I told the Lord I would go, even if I had to return home "in a box." Maybe that's what the Lord was waiting for, because at the last minute a supply of gasoline came in and I was able to get my tank filled plus my canteens for the return trip. I was also able to get Pastor Isaac Keita, another professor at the Bible Institute, to go with me. We would leave the other problems in the Lord's hands.

We left early the next morning, and not too far down the road we came to a bridge that was out, not that big one we had heard about. Is God testing our faith? The workmen were there fixing the bridge, and I used the wait time to get a much-needed nap. I awoke greatly refreshed for the rest of the trip. As we got nearer to the big bridge that we knew was out, we learned of a possible detour, a small bush road that would add quite a few more kilometers to our trip, but it would mean that we could arrive at our destination in our own vehicle.

We stopped to pray before getting on that back road, asking the Lord to guide us and not let us go too far if we shouldn't take this detour. About half a kilometer down the road, we came to a little wooden one-way bridge, with a big truck sitting right in the middle of it. The driver had gone to find someone to come and repair his truck.

We thanked the Lord for answered prayer and left the detour road to drive to the village where we had to leave our vehicle in a pastor's yard. We got a ride on a passing truck that was taking people to the big bridge that was out. There, we used the little temporary footbridge that had been built to get us over the river. On the other side there was already a truck waiting for passengers going to the city of N'Zérékoré.

The truck stopped in front of the church, and the people rushed out to greet us. What a joyous reception! We were late, but we were there, praise the Lord. We went right into the church for our first service. Again, I didn't know how the Lord was going to work things out for me, because I had no voice. But right there was a fellow with a boom box and a microphone – God's answer! And that's how I was able to minister at this Easter conference at the church in N'Zérékoré.

God blessed His Word, in spite of my inadequate condition. I believe that there were eight young people who felt called to the ministry at that conference, and who later came to the Telekoro Bible Institute to study and prepare to serve the Lord. I felt so blessed to be able to witness and be a part of what the Lord was doing in that southern part of the church in Guinea.

And I felt so much better. My voice returned and I didn't have to go back home "in a box!"

THE LONG WAY BACK

THE TRIP HOME after that wonderful Easter in N'Zérékoré wasn't filled with apprehension as was the trip down, but it still took us twenty-four hours. We said our goodbyes at the church and waited for a passing truck that would take us to the big bridge. We crossed the familiar foot-bridge, carrying our luggage, and waited for a ride back to where we left our car.

That truck filled up fairly quickly, but the driver seemed to be waiting for even more riders. I usually try to sit right at the back of the truck. This is so that if the truck leaves the road and goes down into a ravine, which sometimes happens, I can jump out of the truck at the top and not take my chances at the bottom! At least that's how I thought about it.

I was sitting right at the back of the truck waiting to leave. A guy came running up to the back of the truck, wanting to get in. He got one leg in, but the ladies sitting on the middle seat wouldn't move over to give him room to sit. "No room, no room!" they said. The man kept begging them to move over so that he could get in. All they would say was "No room!"

Finally, when there was a lull in his pleading and the chatter in the truck, I said rather loudly so everybody could hear, "My brother, it looks as if we only have room in this truck for your one leg that is already in. I suggest that we cut off your leg so that we can be on our way and you can wait for the next truck to take the rest of you." There was a silent pause followed by hilarious laughter. Apparently, everybody thought it was funny, the ladies moved over, the man got in and sat down, and the rest of the trip was full of friendly banter and laughter.

We arrived where my car was parked and a pastor there asked if we could drop him off at his village on our way, so we headed out. When we arrived at his village, the pastor begged us to stay for something to eat. I looked at Pastor Isaac, and he agreed. Then we saw the kids chasing a rooster, our lunch-to-be! A few hours later, after enjoying a delicious meal that was prepared just for us, we were on the road again. The day was getting longer, but this was Africa!

It was already dark when we drove into a village on the way. A fellow in the middle of the road waved us down. Beyond him was a small truck lying on its side, and the fellow thought we were a bigger vehicle that could pull it back up on its wheels. Pastor Isaac told him, "You don't need a truck. There are enough people around to push the vehicle back upright." The guy didn't think so, so I asked Isaac to go over and get the guys together and get it done. It didn't take him that long, but after Isaac came back, and we were ready to leave, the same guy came to thank us and to tell us that they still needed a truck to pull the vehicle back into the road. I guess it didn't have a starter. Isaac went back again, got the people together to push the vehicle and get it started.

It was after eleven p.m. when Isaac said, "Hey, we're just passing by the village where our friend, Daniel, is the pastor." I said, "It's after eleven, should we stop and see him?" "Why not!" Isaac agreed. So, I made a U-turn and we returned to Daniel's village. A fellow with a rifle met us as we entered the darkened village. "What are you doing here?" this guard asked. "We've come to see Pastor Daniel," we told him. "Follow me," was all this sentry said as he clomped ahead of us.

A knock on the door brought a question from Daniel, "Who is it?" And the sentry gave his own name. When Daniel lit a lantern and opened the door, he saw Isaac and said in amazement, "Pastor Isaac!" Then he saw me and said, "Mr Paul? Wait, what's happened?" Isaac explained that we were just passing by and thought we should stop in and say Hello! It was 11:30 p.m.

Daniel invited us in, lit more lamps, and people from his congregation began to come in. Great fellowship! But then we heard a horn blowing and I asked, "Does that mean what I think it does?" Isaac nodded. And I said, "It's almost midnight and we're going to have a service?!!"

Pretty soon Pastor Daniel told us it was time to head to the church. The church was already full and the service began with congregational singing, just like a normal Sunday morning service! I looked at Isaac and asked, "Are we going to have to speak?" When he said, "Yes," I told him he had to go first, because I was still thinking about what I was going to say.

After the singing, the pastor said, "And now we'll listen to God's Word. Who's going first?" Isaac got up and, as usual, spoke eloquently. When it came my turn, God gave me words, and I spoke about God's family. Though this was the first time they had ever seen me and I them, I said that we were family – God's family, with a special bond, faith in Jesus Christ. It was a special time together, and we weren't in a hurry to leave. We were given a moonlight visit to the poured foundation of the new church they were building there in the village.

It was after 1:00 a.m. when we were finally able to leave the village, and we quickly arrived at the village where we had made a U-turn almost three hours before. To our amazement there was a large crowd milling around the barrier in the middle of the road. Fortunately, the man who came to the car window "happened" to be a relative of Isaac. He explained that when we made the U-turn to go back to see Pastor Daniel, the guards on duty there assumed that we must be evil-doers trying to escape arrest and punishment. Isaac explained who we were, where we were coming from, and why we had made that U-turn. We thanked the Lord for His deliverance as we headed out of that village.

It was well after daylight when we arrived home at the Telekoro Bible Institute, tired but filled with praise to the Lord for all that He had done in making this trip possible. It was a great blessing to us and to many others.

THE ROMANIAN SKEPTIC

A FTER THE END of WWII, the African colonies under European control began to push for independence. France, for its part, came up with a plan for a semi-autonomous relationship and held a yes-or-no vote in her African colonies. They all voted "yes" except for Guinea, which voted 100% "no". So, the French pulled out, taking their vehicles, equipment and household goods with them.

The man elected to be president of Guinea after the French left, Ahmed Sekou Touré, had been schooled in Russia, so his regime established a socialist-style rule for Guinea modelled after the Soviet Union. That regime lasted for 26 years until his death in 1984. As a result, there were lots of Russians, Chinese, and other people from Soviet satellite countries in Europe, living in the Guinean capital city of Conakry, as well as in some smaller centers.

One of these, a Romanian dentist, was assigned to Dalaba, a small community near where our Alliance vacation facility had been established since the 1920s. And it was only 60 kilometers from Mamou where our kids went to school. Florine and I were alone there enjoying a few days of solitude and nature. We heard that the dentist's wife had returned to Romania for family reasons, and that the dentist was alone and the only other foreigner in the area. Florine felt sorry for him, and so we invited him to come for dinner. I picked him up to bring him to our place and he noticed some tracts in the car. He exclaimed, "Oh, what are these?" I told him to take one, that it would be good for him to read it. He began to read, and realizing it was a religious tract, he put it down briskly, exclaiming indignantly, "Bah, I don't need this – this is no good!"

After a good dinner, he left the table with a loud burp, and settled into a comfortable chair. He then launched into a diatribe (in his limited French) against Christianity and all Christians. He pointed up with his finger and declared that he didn't need "Him," that he was rowing his own boat on the sea of life and that was all he needed.

I let him wind down and then said, "Doctor, if you are right and I am wrong, I haven't lost anything. I've lived a good life that honors my God and that tries to help and provide comfort and truth for my fellow man. So, I haven't lost anything. But, Doctor, if I am right and you are wrong, you've lost everything – in this life and the next." All I remember the doctor saying, with a sweep of his hand, was, "Bah!" And he didn't say much on the ride home!

We never saw the doctor again, but I hope that the Holy Spirit used the tract and the brief encounter he had with us to soften his heart and open his mind to the Lord's message of salvation.

"Brothers, my heart's desire and prayer to God for them
is that they may be saved."
Romans 10:1

A TODDLER'S PERSPECTIVE

WE ARRIVED IN Guinea in March 1955, after our one year of language study in France. We were stationed at Faranah, at the old mission station where I grew up. The station had been unoccupied for a number of years but served as a way station for missionaries passing through. There was a brick wall around the back of the building and a lime hedge around the front. A Guinean employee kept the grounds presentable.

David was about two years old when we arrived in Faranah. He had the whole enclosed back yard to play in, but there turned out to be a problem – snakes – and in Africa most snakes are poisonous. We felt a little more secure, however, because there were chickens in the chicken coop, several ducks running around, a pair of guinea fowl also loose, and a pet monkey, all with excellent eyesight for snakes.

One day David was playing alone in the back yard when he began to cry. I looked out the window and said, "What's the matter, David?" He replied, "The guinea rooster pecked me." Well, the guinea rooster was indeed right in front of him but was facing away from him. I noticed that it was pecking at something on the ground about three feet away from David. I ran out to find that it was a carpet viper that the rooster was attacking, a small, but very poisonous viper. We killed the snake, gave it to the ducks to eat, and praised the Lord for His marvelous protection for our son and for us. We killed at least sixty snakes on our property during the first year, and two of them in the house.

David had a little playmate, a girl named Terna. She was the daughter of our yardman, Saa. She had an older brother, Mamadi, but he was too old to play with David. Besides, he didn't wear any clothes, which at that time was quite typical for African boys until they reached puberty. Girls also didn't wear much, but they often had a loin cloth, a small patch of cloth suspended in front from the beads around their waist. All girls and women wear beads around the waist as a fertility thing. Anyway, we asked that Terna wear more clothes when she came to play with David, so she usually came in bloomers. They spent quite a bit of time playing together with David's toys in the sand box.

Playing with the "locals" is a great way to learn the language, and David was growing up bi-lingual. I also grew up bi-lingual, so I didn't have a problem returning to Guinea, except for the grammar! But Florine was starting from scratch. She thought that David, even at his tender age, could maybe help her learn the language. But all David would say when she tried to say something in Maninka was, "Mommy, you talk funny."

A Guinean who came to see me once heard David and Terna playing in the sand box, and he said about David," If you didn't see who it was that was talking, you would think he was one of our kids."

I drove to the village of Yatia one Sunday morning to preach at the church there. It was a trip of about 18 miles, and we had to cross the Niger River on a ferry. I took David and Terna with me. Terna's Aunt Fatumata was the pastor's wife, and I assumed that she would take care of the two kids. At the church I sat on a bench at the front along the side, and Fatumata sat on a bench opposite me, with the two kids beside her and her nursing baby on her lap. And, of course, this nursing mother had no top on. Sometime before I was due to get up to speak, I saw Terna reach up, get ahold of her aunt's breast and take a swig. Nothing unusual there. But then she pointed the breast at David, offering him a taste too. I sat a few moments with trepidation, wondering just what he was going to do, since he and Terna usually did everything together. He finally shook his head, and the service continued for me.

Our first term at Faranah was an interesting time for us. Quite a few people remembered me as a child. They couldn't address me now as "Paul," so they called me Mr. Paul, instead of Mr. Ellenberger. Florine became Madame Paul. And in the local African fashion, Guinean friends would drop by just to say hello.

A man stopped by one day and found me in the back yard, lying on a mat under our pickup truck doing some mechanical work. David, three years old or so, was on his back right beside me. After the necessary "Hello, how are you?" the visitor said, "Mr. Paul, isn't the child in your way?" I pulled myself out from under the car and said to him, "I know what you would say. 'Get out of here, this is no work for a child.'" He agreed with me. I continued, "Then when your boy is 15 years old, you will say to him, 'Come here, son, hold this pencil and learn to write.' But you know, my son is watching what I do, and before long I will be able to call out to him, 'Son, hand me the hammer or the wrench,' and he will know how to help me without my having to go after what I need. And he will learn to fix the car, too!"

David continued to develop a strong interest in mechanical work throughout his childhood and teenage years. He ultimately attended an aviation school in Utica, New York, and after graduation, moved to Florida. He started out at a small airport doing general aviation work on small, private planes. He worked as a structural mechanic at Eastern Airlines and finished his career at American Airlines as an avionics technician. He just retired after 40 years of working in this field. I would say he had a good start lying under that pickup truck all those years ago!

Church at Faranah with attached residence. Paul lived here as a young boy with his family in the 1930s, and then again in the mid50s with Florine and David.

Toddler David

125

THE POLICE CHASE

AFTER THE '67 crisis in Guinea and the expulsion of most of our missionary staff, our Mamou Alliance Academy, which I attended in 1931-1939, and which our children also attended, had to be closed in 1971. Our remaining primary and secondary students transferred to Kabala Rupp Memorial School in Kabala, Sierra Leone, and the high school students went to Ivory Coast Academy (ICA) in Bouake, Ivory Coast (now Cote d'Ivoire). ICA was operated by another mission, but the C&MA helped with staff and support.

In 1978, our daughter Sandie was graduating from ICA, and we were planning to drive to Ivory Coast to attend her graduation. This was quite a challenge. Because of the political situation, there was only limited travel between our countries, and our unpaved roads were not kept up very well.

We left the Bible School early in the morning, hoping to be able to get to Bamako, Mali, to spend the night at the mission there. But the road was so bad, in places covered with water, that I didn't dare drive through without first wading through on foot. We didn't reach the Guinea border until 9:00 p.m. The head customs officer had already retired for the night and wouldn't respond to my knocking. And it was he who had to sign our passports.

I drove to an unpopulated area of bush where we could park and spend the night in the car. Karyn had the back seat, and Florine and I reclined in the front seats. We lit a mosquito coil and put it on the dash.

In the morning, we arrived at the border office before the head customs officer had finished brushing his teeth in the back yard. He came into the office, made no apologies or any reference to our having to spend the night in the car. He signed our passports, and we were on our way to Cote d'Ivoire, through Mali.

Driving a car with Guinea license plates brought quite a bit of attention in Cote d'Ivoire. Policemen there stopped us just to see if we were really from that socialist country of Guinea. They had never seen a vehicle from Guinea before!

We enjoyed Sandie's graduation and all the activities there at Ivory Coast Academy. We started our journey towards home, and soon learned our return trip to Guinea would be more exciting than we had anticipated!

We left Cote d'Ivoire and were cutting across the corner of Burkina Faso. The road was good, and we were enjoying the ride, until we came to a police checkpoint. A policeman was there directing us to stop. Just then, another vehicle, loaded with passengers and roof-top baggage, and a driver's apprentice who was also sitting up on the roof-top, came from behind us. The policeman kept blowing his whistle, but the vehicle kept right on going. The policeman came back to our car, opened the rear door, and jumped in beside Sandie and Karyn. He said to me in a commanding voice, "Follow that vehicle!"

I started driving as fast as I felt was safe, to catch up to the vehicle we were pursuing. When we got near to it, the policeman ordered me to pull up beside the vehicle. As I did so, my girls said in a rather urgent voice, "Dad, he's got a gun!" And I told them to just keep down and out of his way. As I pulled up beside the traveling vehicle, the policeman extended his arm in front of the girls, pointing his gun out the window at the driver and yelled, "Stop your vehicle!"

The driver finally obeyed, and I was ordered to pass and then stop in front of the vehicle. The policeman jumped out, did a three-point spread on the hood of that car, pointing his revolver right at the driver, ordering him to shut off the motor. When he felt he had things under control, he came back to our car and said in an official voice, "You may now proceed." I thanked him, and we left as he was getting in the other vehicle, which had to return to the check point.

I guess my one and only police chase was successful. I wondered how much explaining the driver had to do back at the checkpoint. We thanked the Lord for keeping us safe and providing Sandie and Karyn with a good story!

THE ERRANT MACHETE

AFTER DAVID, OUR first son, stayed in the States to finish high school, his brother, Keith, inherited full use of my .22 rifle. While Keith was on vacation from boarding school, the student wives at the Telekoro Bible Institute really appreciated him. When he returned from hunting, he would pass through the student quarters and donate what game he had managed to shoot.

Keith also loved to join student work crews and help maintain the tidy appearance of the school property. One day the crew was cutting back some underbrush with machetes, and Keith was helping them. With his left hand, he held the brush to be cut off, and suddenly his machete slashed higher than he intended and sliced four fingers on the inside of his left hand, the fourth finger very deeply. There was a lot of blood and the workman closest to him put pressure on his bleeding finger as they walked together to the dispensary.

Peggy Harvey, our nurse, tried to stop the bleeding and bandaged the wound, but the cut on that ring finger was so deep that we had to take him in to the hospital in Kissidougou. They stitched the wound and sent him home. His finger eventually healed.

A few years later we returned to the U.S. for our furlough, and the doctor said Keith would need surgery to repair his index finger. Though the ring finger had been severely cut, the tendon on his index finger had been severed and Keith could not bend that joint. It needed to be repaired to restore full use of his finger. We assumed this would be a fairly simple procedure.

We took Keith to a surgeon up near Buffalo, NY, and learned that the surgery was far more complicated than what we had thought. Because the injury had happened more than three years before, the ends of the severed tendon had pulled quite far apart. The surgeon said he would have to find a piece of tendon in the wrist or somewhere else, that could be used to reconnect the severed tendon in Keith's index finger. And even if this were done, he reminded us, it would not necessarily insure the full use of the finger. If we opted to not do the surgery, the surgeon recommended a procedure to freeze the finger in a bent position. Otherwise, left untreated it would eventually bend back unnaturally, rendering it difficult to use and open to breaking.

We did some fast praying about what to do. God had gifted Keith with a lot of musical abilities. He played the piano, the guitar and the ukulele, and he needed the use of that finger. If it was bent in a permanent position, it would no doubt impair those abilities. God could enable the surgeon's operating skills to restore the use of Keith's finger. We decided to move forward with the surgery.

In the waiting room we prayed and waited. And as the waiting time lengthened, we were beginning to wonder if we had made the right decision.

Finally, it was over and we were able to see Keith. Were we surprised! His left hand was wrapped in bandages, his left wrist was bandaged, as were his right hand and right foot. When the surgeon came in, he explained that he had a hard time finding a piece of tendon long enough to make the repair to that index finger. Nothing from the left or right wrist would work, but he was able to find a piece of tendon from the right foot that was long enough.

It was pretty discouraging for us to see all that Keith had been through. And even then, the surgeon couldn't guarantee that Keith's finger would be completely usable again as before. But our trust was in God.

We returned to our ministry in Guinea and Keith stayed in the U.S. to finish high school. Before leaving, we were able to take him for a follow-up appointment with the surgeon. He finally confirmed that Keith's operation was successful, and that he would regain the use of that finger. What a testimony of God's power to that surgeon, and to us!

Keith made a full recovery, and God has blessed and used his musical gifts on the mission field and on home assignment ministries.

Fast forward forty-five years. Keith and his wife, Krista were now serving in Bomako, Mali. Keith had the privilege of driving the C&MA president and his team to Kankan, Guinea, in January 2019 for the 100th celebration of the C&MA national church. He was able to meet many believers who had had an impact on our family. Keith relayed the story to me. "As I was greeting a group of white-haired men and women, one short man asked me, 'Do you remember who I am?' I looked carefully and intently at his face, trying to bring up something from my past experiences of growing up in Guinea, but nothing was coming. He then said, 'I am the guy who saved your life.' I knew immediately who it was, because I have never forgotten that day. He was the one who put pressure on my bleeding finger and walked with me to the dispensary. I was quite emotional as I gave him a big hug and said, 'Yes, you did save my life that day! Thank you again!'"

*Keith's provision to one of the students
(which probably went into a wonderful sauce!)*

132

MY FIRST FRENCH LESSON

WE HAD JUST moved into the Villa Emmanuel in Mornex, France in 1954 to begin our French language study. The larger town of Annemasse was down the mountain near the large Lake Leman, which the Swiss liked to call Lake Geneva.

There was bus service that passed through our village going down to Annemasse, so I thought I would check things out to see what all was available. I was having a good time looking around and getting oriented. Since I had to wait awhile for a bus going back to the Villa, I decided to find a bathroom - couldn't wait until I got home! I looked high and low around the town square for a public toilet. I remembered that in Paris there were public "pissoirs" (public places for men to relieve themselves) and, while I needed to make a more substantial contribution, I couldn't even find one of those!

In growing distress, I found a local policeman and asked him, in my limited French, where I could find the "toilette." That sounded French, and I figured he would at least get the idea of what I needed. He looked at me, frowning and said repeatedly "Toilette? Toilette? Toilette?" I saw that he had no idea what I was asking for, or at least why I was asking for a toilette. Remembering the letters "WC" on the toilet doors back at the Villa, I ventured again with a French accent, "The double-V–C." In French, the letter W is pronounced like a "V." I thought there could be no mistaking that!

But again, I got the same results. "Double-V–C? Double-V–C? Double-V–C?" Then the policeman added in French, "Really? Double-V–C? Good gracious! I have no idea."

And he hunched his shoulders in that typical French gesture of incomprehension.

I was becoming desperate, especially thinking about how long I had yet to wait for my bus to come. All of a sudden, the Frenchman exploded in understanding, "Ahhhhhhhh, le VC, le VC – c'est juste la-bas Monsieur," as he triumphantly pointed to a small sign not too far away. "Merci beaucoup, Monsieur" probably wasn't commensurate with his exercise of understanding a foreigner, but I was much relieved, in more ways than one!

By the way, to a Frenchman, the "toilette" (twa-let) is a dressing room, maybe with a washstand, but never a toilet as we refer to it. And the "VC" is the popular way the French refer to the toilet, by using an English name, water closet, or WC, with a French accent!

Ahhhhhhhh. . . My first French lesson!

TWO UNLIKELY PASTORS

THE BIBLE INSTITUTE initially only provided training in the Maninka language. Over time, the courses were offered in both Maninka and French. When the national schools adopted French, the Institute phased out the Maninka courses and transitioned the entire program to the French language.

Elijah was one of the last Telekoro Bible Institute students to graduate in the Maninka language. Elijah was quiet, unassuming, a poor student, and not very likely to succeed in the ministry. His wife was in Florine's class for women, and usually sat on the floor, a twin nursing at each breast, trying to write on the floor somehow between them. I gave Elijah a final grade of "D" just to ease him out and yet give him a chance in the ministry. I was sure that he wouldn't amount to much. Elijah and his wife were placed at a church in a remote area, and we heard they were having a rough time.

Quite some time later I received a letter from Elijah. "Mr. Paul, we've built a new church here. Would you please come and dedicate it for us?" I was smitten! I had written him off, and yet God had used him and blessed his ministry and helped him prosper. Some other students of mine who were smart, capable and most promising, and for whom I had every hope of good success, lasted only a brief time in ministry. Humbly, I went to dedicate this new church. They had built a mud structure with a tin roof and there were at least 100 people attending and the congregation was still growing! I found out that, while building this church, Elijah was also regularly visiting another village at quite some distance away and establishing a church there.

Peter was another student of mine who graduated from the Telekoro Bible Institute. He was pastoring a church in another remote area. My private name for Peter while at school was "Squeaky," because he had a rather high-pitched voice. He was a "character," a joker and a talker. One New Year's Eve, Peter and a group from his church were on their way to another village to hold a service, when he collapsed, probably from a stroke. Those with him carried him back to their village.

I became involved when the district superintendent came and asked me if I would drive out to the village and bring Peter back to his own home village to recuperate. It was one of those roads that can hardly be called a road, with rocks, ruts, and streams to cross, with no bridge, etc. Anyway, I got him back to his home village and he began to slowly get better.

Now, back to Elijah and the extension village that he walked to every week. The group of Christians there grew and developed, and they eventually built a church and sent a letter to the district superintendent asking for a pastor. The DS responded, "We don't have a pastor to send to you," to which this new church replied, "We don't care if you don't have a pastor to send to us. We want one anyway."

Peter, who was recovering in his village from the stroke, heard about the church that needed a pastor, and wrote to the DS. "If you don't have anyone else to send to that village, I'll go. I can't walk, and I can't visit neighboring villages, but I can sit and teach the people God's Word and they can sit and listen." The new church was informed about this possibility and the people were elated. They had a pastor. The road to that village was terrible, so a tractor pulling a trailer took Peter and his family to his new charge.

But Peter eventually became very discouraged. There were too many villages, too many people that needed to hear about Jesus, and he couldn't just sit there. He went to preach in a nearby village, accompanied by a group from his church. On the way, he passed out. When he came to, members of his group were praying over him, "Lord, don't let our pastor die!" Peter told them that he was okay, and they were to go ahead and let the folks know that he was coming. "When I get my legs, I'll be there," was his explanation. Peter ministered there for a year or so before the Lord took him home.

How many people heard about Jesus because of these two faithful servants, Elijah and Peter!

I ARREST YOU

D AVID AND HEIDI came to Guinea to visit and we finally got to spend time with our first grandchild, Kristen, then about a year old. They had come before when she was 6 months old, but due to some other circumstances, we didn't get to spend time together.

This time they were able to accompany us on our monthly trip to Gbenko, a diamond mining site that was not too far from the Telekoro Bible Institute. At this mining site, there were a number of European expatriates involved with the mining operation, and we went there monthly for a Christian ministry in English, usually spending an overnight.

The road we had to take part way to Gbenko was not paved then, and there were some bad spots that we had to pass on our way. David, who grew up in Guinea, was used to roads like this, but now he had a video camera to be able to record some of it.

We were riding in our Dodge Crew Cab air-conditioned pickup, so our windows were up and we were enjoying family conversation. All of a sudden, I was aware that a public transportation vehicle was driving right along beside me. A police officer, who was riding in the front passenger seat, was pointing out his window at me and trying to tell me something. I quickly told David to put down his camera, and I rolled my window down.

The policeman asked me in French, "What are you doing?" to which I just said, "What?" The policeman then said, "I arrest you," and I said, trying to be nice, "Thank you very much." And I rolled my window back up and kept on driving.

The poor policeman couldn't make me stop, and the driver, who obviously didn't want to get involved, passed me and kept on going.

During the previous socialist regime, no pictures were allowed to be taken in Guinea. Even though this was years later, it was hard for the police and other authority figures to forget that things had changed and taking pictures was really okay now.

Paul and David, with the "questionable" camera!

I KNOW SOMEONE FROM AFRICA

AFTER WWII AND my return to the U.S., I stayed with my
Grandma Patterson in Flint, Michigan. The most direct route back
and forth to Houghton College was across Ontario, Canada, crossing
into Canada at Buffalo and entering Michigan at Sarnia. That meant
crossing the border twice, but it usually went smoothly and quickly
for Americans.

On this particular trip back to Michigan, I crossed Canada and
arrived at the U.S. border in the afternoon. The U.S. customs officer
posed the usual first question, "Where were you born?" I answered,
"Africa," and expected the next obvious question to be about my nation-
ality. But he totally surprised me by saying, "Africa, I know somebody from Africa." And he kept saying, "What was his name?" Then he
explained that fifteen years ago, he was a customs officer at the Port
Authority of New York City, and this missionary family came in from
Africa. He kept racking his brain, saying "What was his name?" Of
course, I'm thinking that there are several thousand American missionaries in Africa and that even if he ever came up with his name, I
wouldn't know him anyway. But he kept trying to remember the name,
and I was eager to be on my way to Flint.

Then, all of a sudden, the light came on and he said triumphantly,
"FRED!" And I asked, "Joder?" And he said excitedly, "Yes, that's it,
Fred Joder!"

I couldn't believe it! I knew the Joders. They were C&MA missionaries serving in French West Africa, and two of their children attended
the same MK school that I did.

Think of the odds! But more than that, think of a man doing his job in New York with all the people that he meets every day, and fifteen years later he can remember this missionary's name! Fred and his family must have made quite an impression on this man. I drove away reflecting on the impact one missionary had on an immigration agent. Lord, make me like Fred Yoder.

GOLDILOCKS AND THE
THREE CUBANS

KARYN WAS A teenager and the last of our four children with us
on the field. I had purchased a motorcycle in the U.S., a Kawasaki
100 off-road bike, to bring back to Africa. It would help me get around
the large Telekoro Bible School campus, especially for taking care of
the maintenance. Karyn took a liking to this bike while she was on
vacation from Kabala Rupp Memorial School (KRMS). She drove this
motorcycle all over the place, down to the rice paddies, over the har-
vested peanut hills for the off-road effect, and to the various villages
in the area. Everybody recognized her, and many would tell me about
seeing her on the moto, the local term for a motorcycle.

One day, at the beginning of our new school year at the Telekoro
Bible School, I received a note from some married students who were
on their way from the Kankan direction with their families. The truck
they were coming on had broken down. They were hoping that I would
come and get them.

I was getting the Mission van ready when Karyn found out about it
and asked if she could go along on the motorcycle. I told her that the
distance, maybe 25 miles or so, was too far for her to ride the moto,
but that I would put a plank in the van, and when I thought she had
ridden far enough, I would stop and use the plank for her to drive the
moto up into the van.

We came across the broken-down truck with our students and
families, and I went about getting them and their stuff loaded into the

van. Karyn came before we were ready to leave and asked if she could go on ahead, and I would pick her up when we caught up with her. It sounded like a good plan and she took off.

When I had everything and everybody loaded, we headed back toward the Bible School. I wasn't sure how far Karyn would get before we caught up with her. As we rounded a curve, there she was, stopped at the side of the road, and on the other side of the road was a parked Cuban army truck. The Cuban army was involved in paving the road between Kissidougou and Kankan, and they were notorious for using local women for their pleasure. There were three Cuban men in the truck cab, and I pulled up and greeted them in French.

"She's out of gas," the driver told me. I said, "No, she has enough gas." I said to Karyn, in English, "That little gas valve under the seat that you switch on when you start the moto, turn it back the other way. That's your gas reserve. Then kick it to get it started, and get out of here." She did that, got it started and took off. I thanked the Cubans for their concern for my daughter, though I still wonder what they were really thinking . . . finding a beautiful blonde out in the middle of nowhere!

I went home and told Florine about Goldilocks and the three Cubans.

A FIRST FOR SANDINYA

FRANCE GAINED CONTROL of what was called French West Africa by 1900. There were few roads and, of course, few cars. The French government set about in those early years to push roads through the jungle. They did this with forced labor, enlisting work teams from around the villages where the new road would pass. Even in the 1930s, new roads were being opened. Passing vehicles were not very common, and a lot of local people had never even seen a motor vehicle.

A new road had just opened beyond Yatia, the village where Dad had built an "outstation." We had a mission house and a church building there. Another large village, Sandinya, had just been reached by the new road, and Dad wanted to preach the Gospel there for the first time.

One Sunday after the service at the Yatia church, Dad got a small group together and drove on the new road toward Sandinya. And, of course, I went along. As we neared the town, there was a long stretch where the road was straight, something not too usual in the jungle.

Way up ahead, we could see a couple walking toward the village on this new road. The man was walking ahead, using a walking stick. His wife followed along behind him, carrying a fairly large load on her head, a typical scene in Africa.

As we got closer, we could see when the noise of our approaching vehicle reached these walkers. The woman slowly turned, holding on to the load on her head. When she saw this "thing" coming at them, she quickly dumped her load, ran up to the man and gave him a big shove.

He disappeared into the thick, tall grass at the side of the road. Then she dove in after him.

As we drove by, the man and woman each parted the grass and were peering out to see what this thing was that was passing by — probably the first car they had ever seen! The Christians in our vehicle thought this was hilarious.

The people of Sandinya heard the Gospel for the first time that day and received it with open hearts!

A COURAGEOUS LITTLE GIRL

BIYO (BEE-YO) WAS a six-year-old girl whose parents "loaned" her to relatives, an Aunt and Uncle who were studying at the Telekoro Bible Institute. This is consistent with tribal practice for the training of a young girl to do housework, take care of babies and younger children, and do other chores. Biyo had time to play with the other kids at the Bible Institute and run around the campus.

On Saturday mornings during the school term, we would make a run with the school van into Kissidougou, our nearest town center. The students could shop at the market, sell some things, or take care of necessary business. The van would return around noon with mostly student wives who had been food-shopping.

It was my turn to drive the van on this particular Saturday, and as we returned to the campus, a group of children were there awaiting their parents' return. Our German shepherd dog also ran down to greet us. Biyo was apparently scared by the big dog and jumped out in front of the van, just as I was bringing it to a stop. I heard the thud and stopped as quickly as possible, without having really seen anyone because of the cab-over characteristic of this vehicle.

One of the students pulled Biyo out from behind the front wheel and laid her inert body by the side of the road. I was devastated! I had run over this little girl! She was motionless and I assumed that she was dead. Her one thigh was visibly broken, her foot facing the wrong way, so I moved her leg and saw her eyes blink. She's not dead, I remember thinking. She had to be rushed to the hospital. Fortunately, another missionary took charge, got Biyo and her aunt into the car and rushed in to the hospital.

Thus began a long, painful story. The hospital usually closes around noontime, but the doctor was there and was able to set Biyo's thigh, although he didn't have everything needed to make a proper cast. Her mother and father were informed and came as quickly as possible from their village. Biyo's mother had a nursing baby, so she stayed with her at the hospital for the next five or six months.

The morning after the accident I was called in by the Chief of Police to meet with him and Biyo's father. The Chief didn't mince any words. "This white man has killed your daughter. How much do you want?" I'm sitting there wondering what this man is going to say. The father, puzzled by what the Chief said, replied, "But she's not dead!" To which the Police Chief replied, "Well, if you think she's going to make it, you're mistaken. So, how much do you want?"

There was a slight pause, and the father told the Chief with confidence, "I don't want anything. God gave this girl to me to keep and to love, and I've had her for over six years now. If God wants to take her back, that's up to Him. I can only praise Him for letting her be a part of my family." I was amazed by what this father said; he was a Christian of great faith. The Police Chief was left almost speechless and he told me that it was now my responsibility to take care of Biyo and her family. And that was a job I had to accept with faith and confidence.

At the hospital Biyo had a small room with one bed. She was in the bed and her mother slept on a mat on the floor beside the bed with her baby, and she did this for several months. I usually went to town daily to see Biyo and her mother, pay the bills, and give the mother money for food and other expenses. But I thanked the Lord for sparing Biyo's life, for a Christian father and mother, and for God's healing hand to be on Biyo's leg.

One day our missionary nurse went to see Biyo, and she returned quite shaken. It appeared that the doctor was having a hard time because the cast was not strong enough to keep Biyo's thigh bone in the proper position for it to bond and heal. The hospital nurse had hung a five-kilo (ten pound) weight on her foot at the end of the bed to keep her leg straight. Our nurse told me that that much weight on the foot was stopping the blood circulation and they would soon have to amputate her foot. I made a wooden brace to hold the foot in its proper position, and that seemed to work very well.

Biyo was finally released from the hospital, and I drove her and her mother to Conakry, the capital, to have the hip x-rayed and to have a consultation with a specialist, a surgeon from East Germany. The leg was healing well, though not yet completely. The surgeon wanted us to bring her back in a couple of months because the bone was not properly butted, but overlapped. He would operate by re-breaking the bone and re-setting it properly.

When we returned to Kissidougou and delivered the x-rays and the surgeon's recommendations, Biyo's doctor would only say, "It's well-knit together." And he went on to say that re-breaking it and doing it all over again would open it up to infection and more problems that we didn't need. "I like it like this," he concluded.

Biyo's mother's main concern was that because of the broken thigh bone and all that had happened, Biyo would never be able to have a baby. In Africa that is all-important. Biyo went home to the village with her parents, and we didn't see her again for a few years.

We returned to Guinea in 1996 for the 50th Anniversary celebration of the Telekoro Bible Institute. That's where we heard that Biyo was now married, had two healthy children and was expecting her third! Praise the Lord! God is so good!

THE POWER OF LANGUAGE

FLORINE AND I retired in 1990, after 36 years of ministry in Guinea. About that time, a civil war broke out in Liberia, a neighboring country to Guinea, and about 400,000 refugees pushed into Guinea. It was a tribal conflict between tribal groups in Liberia. The pagan Mano and Gio tribes fought against the Islamized Krahn and Mandingo tribes. The hatred was intense, and many fleeing refugees were slaughtered.

The Red Cross International provides aid for refugees but works through the local Red Cross agency. In this situation, the Mandingos of Guinea were the dominant tribe and had more control over the local Red Cross and its decisions. They refused to give help to certain people, especially Christians. They also let many locals, non-refugees, sign up to receive the rations that were given out to refugees by the Red Cross.

The Christian & Missionary Alliance has a ministry called CAMA Services, which was founded to help refugees worldwide. In 1991 they sent Al and Beth Bosenburg to Guinea to help the Christians and others that were being neglected by the war. I was asked to go along and help. While this was a challenging ministry, it was also very rewarding.

The village of Péla was one place I had to visit to see about the distribution of rations. I had heard that the local Red Cross leaders had listed almost nine thousand refugees in that area, and I knew there couldn't possibly be that many. So, I hired a Christian refugee (I will call him John in this story) to go out and take a census of the refugees there. I had to visit somewhere else in the meantime, and when

I returned to the administrative center, I found that my hired census taker had been arrested.

When I went to see the chief of police to get John released, I found that this policeman was a former student of mine from the Bible school where we taught for many years. I asked him why he had put my man in jail, and he said that it was because he was re-doing what the local Red Cross had "officially" done. He had declared there were only 1,319 real refugees, when the Red Cross had reported there were 8,769.

I was speaking with the police chief in French. But there happened to be two Red Cross men in the back of the room who didn't speak French and who wanted to know what we were talking about. They spoke in the Maninka language and didn't know that I spoke that language from my childhood.

The chief switched to Maninka and told them that I was complaining that the Red Cross count of refugees was way too high, that it included so many local non-refugees. They replied, "That's not true," and went on to justify their count. It went back and forth like that until I had had enough. I turned to them, switched to Maninka, and read them the riot act. Their mouths dropped – they couldn't believe their ears!

Well, the police chief released John, and although it probably didn't change anything with the local Red Cross, we went on with our ministry of providing for refugees. All refugees who needed help heard the good news of a loving Savior who was very interested in providing His wonderful saving grace for all people.

MY NAMESAKE

DURING MY THREE-MONTH assignment working with refugees near the Guinea–Liberian border in 1991, I learned that there was another Paul Ellenberger at the nearby village of Nawé.

Nearly three years earlier, I had been the guest speaker at a conference that was held at the area's central church, and a local Christian, Lazarus Loua, had attended that conference. When he arrived home after the conference, he found that his pregnant wife had given birth to a baby boy and was awaiting his return, to give a name to the newborn. He must have been impressed by my ministry at the conference, as he named the boy Paul Ellenberger Loua.

Now, with his village within reach, I was obliged by African custom to visit my namesake, meet his parents, grandparents, uncles, aunts and neighbors. And, of course, that would mean gifts for the boy, his mother and father, as well as for other family members. I had a local helper who went with me to the market in the big city and helped me buy appropriate gifts.

On the day of my visit to Nawé, everybody seemed excited to meet me, except for my three-year-old namesake. He yelled mightily every time I got near him! Of course, I was probably the first white person he had ever seen, and his reaction was understandable, if not always typical.

I had a soccer ball for Paul, which he didn't refuse, bright-colored dresses for his mother, as well as other gifts. I was treated with a fine dinner and given a live young rooster to carry home with me.

I haven't seen Paul Ellenberger Loua since that day. He would be thirty-two years old now as I write this, and I sincerely hope that he is not trying to be like me, but like Jesus, our Savior and Lord.

Paul with his namesake, Paul Ellenberger

155

Paul with his namesake and family

AND THE TWO SHALL BE ONE

REMEMBER HOW I said working with the Liberian refugees was challenging, but also rewarding? One of those very rewarding projects started with my first visit to the refugee camp in Baala. There were about twenty thousand refugees being sheltered there.

Two refugee leaders came to me at separate times to ask for my help. They were pastors of different denominational church groups from Liberia, trying to maintain a ministry with their refugee members. One church group met for services under one tree and the other met under another tree. They wanted me to help them with shelters for their group meetings.

It was my suggestion that, given the circumstances, they get together as one group, which would give them increased ability to build one shelter. There were plenty of smaller trees there that could supply the framework for a structure. I told them I would try to get a couple of tarpaulins to help with the covering for the roof.

Well, the two church groups decided to unite. They were able to build a large thatched shelter with bamboo pole seats and a fixed pulpit. I figured that sixty or more persons could be seated. Pastor Cooper served as the lead pastor, and Pastor Bleedee accepted the role of assistant pastor.

My last visit to this church was shortly before I left Africa for the U.S. It was a Sunday, the bamboo benches were filled, and they asked me to preach. What a delightful service and a definite answer to prayer.

After the service, they had a dinner prepared for everyone. These refugees didn't have much, but they had prepared rice and a leaf gravy with large hunks of pork rind and tripe. I really did enjoy it!

It was indeed a privilege to see how God was working under such difficult circumstances to bring blessing to His people and a needed witness to many others.

Thatched shelter for church

159

Two congregations in front of new church.

THE UNUSUAL COLLECTIBLE

ONE DAY A neighbor who lived near the Telekoro Bible Institute campus came to ask me if I would come and kill the snake that had swallowed his calf. He had tied his cow, with her 6-month-old calf, along our road near the Bible School entrance. He probably thought it would be safer there from being stolen.

I got my .22 rifle and followed him to where the python was hiding under a bush. After a python swallows a large prey, it has difficulty moving and usually hides until everything has been digested and it's able to move freely. This one was well-hidden, with its head on the ground, from where it could see out around it. One shot in the head killed it, but since none of the young men with our neighbor were willing to pull the snake from its place, I had to go after it, finding the tail and pulling it out to its full length. One fellow with a machete chopped off the head before I could stop him. Then he wanted to chop off the tail, to let the life out, he told me.

The snake was now the property of the owner of the calf it had swallowed, and he agreed to let me have the skin for killing it. His young men went to work with their knives, slitting the under belly the length of the snake. They removed the calf, which had to be discarded, and cut the snake meat into sections that the guys could carry home.

By this time, some students from the Bible School had arrived at the scene and helped me carry the wet python skin back to the house. Joseph, the school maintenance man, helped me skin the head and we put the skull in the crotch of a tree to let the ants clean off all the tissue. We pegged the snake skin out flat on the ground to let it dry. I had a friend in town who was a leather worker and who eventually tanned the skin for me and sewed the head skin back onto the body to make it sixteen and a half feet long. It's the only snake skin I've seen that also has the skin from the head with the two eye holes!

Our son David took control of the python's skull. He took the bone structure all apart, cleaning all the bones. When it was put back together, he had a one-of-a-kind skeletal snake head with a light bulb showing the teeth. He hung the snake skull from the ceiling in his bedroom!

For my part, I had a large python skin to display with my other collectibles from West Africa. When I went on missions tours in the U.S., it became quite a subject of conversation. I was at a church in Daytona Beach, Florida, and a man at my display table told me, "Your snake skin needs a treatment." He was a leather worker and said he would treat my snake skin for free. When he brought it back, he asked me if I knew how much this skin was worth. Of course, I had no clue. The figure he gave me made me think that I should no longer leave the skin displayed publicly! But I did. People liked to see it, and they also didn't know how much it was worth!

Karyn with 16-foot
python skin

A LIFE WELL LIVED

OUR FAMILY'S ASSOCIATION with Isaac Keita goes way back. My mother was present at his birth and had the privilege of telling his father that he had a healthy baby boy. The new father, Paul Keita, was one of the first students to enroll at the Bible school started by my parents, Clair and Ruth Ellenberger, in 1945. This school would later be known as the Telekoro Bible Institute.

My mother wrote that Paul was overjoyed at the news that he had a healthy son, since they had lost more than one baby before that. He spent most of that morning looking for an Old Testament name for the boy, something different from the usual Pauls, Peters, and Johns. He settled on Issachar, pronounced popularly as "Sakari" and that was what the boy was called until he went to French school, where they wrote it down as "Isaac" – and Isaac it was from then on.

Isaac spent his first years at the Bible school with his parents. Years later he was to return to the school as a professor, where he poured himself into the formation of other young men and women for the cause of Christ in Guinea. Although a professor at the school, he sat with the students in Florine's English class in order to further his grasp on the English language. This would eventually help him pursue the theological studies that culminated in the conferral of his doctoral degree.

Working with Isaac was always a pleasure. I knew him to be highly capable, yet humble and even-tempered. He truly was a man of God with a passionate love for Jesus and an earnest desire to see lives transformed by the power of God.

Isaac Keita joins a growing list of truly gifted men and women that God has raised up to impact the cause of Christ in Africa. From our human viewpoint, we could feel that his ministry was ended too soon, but we know that the divine prospective gives the true evaluation of a life well lived for the glory of God.

Isaac teaching, Telekoro Bible Institute

LASSA FEVER

FEVERS ARE NOT a new subject to Africa. The ranks of the first Christian and Missionary Alliance missionaries to West Africa, beginning in 1890, were decimated by deadly fevers. Nobody seemed to know much about them back then. There was a lot of yellow fever outbreaks, and malaria, which was spread by mosquitoes. In spite of this, God's servants faithfully filled in the ranks and persevered to plant the church of Jesus Christ in the various countries of French West Africa. The Church grew and developed into vibrant fellowships that continue to extend Christ's kingdom today.

In spite of modern science, fevers still claim their toll. When I was a child growing up in Guinea in the early 1930s, I remember the quarantines in the attempts to control yellow fever. More recently other fever outbreaks have posed problems, in spite of increased vaccinations and the use of quinine and its modern derivatives.

Mrs. Carrie Moore was a missionary widow who lived in a small house just across the driveway from our house at the Telekoro Bible Institute. Mrs. Moore helped translate the New Testament into the Kissi language. In August 1965, she came down with a severe illness and fever that resulted in permanent deafness and loss of all her hair. Then in January 1967, Don Loose, another missionary teacher at the Bible Institute, had a debilitating fever, from which he recovered after a lengthy rehabilitation.

In late January 1968, Florine and I took a long trip to Freetown, Sierra Leone. This was an annual shopping trip for us, to replace supplies which were unavailable in Guinea. On an earlier trip, we had been able to visit the small chapel at Makomp, Sierra Leone, where my dad and mom were married on November 2, 1923.

The long daily activities seemed to take a toll on me, and I remember feeling so exhausted by nighttime that I wondered how I would be able to do anything the next day. But the Lord gave me new energy for each day. The long, two-day trip home to Guinea was taxing. The next morning, however, I was not able to get out of bed. I had fever, with extreme exhaustion and vomiting, symptoms that the others had had. I don't remember how long I remained bed-ridden, but fellow missionaries and national pastors came from far away to pray for me.

Another missionary teacher at the Bible Institute, Dave Harvey, also suffered from this fever in April-May 1969. By that time the illness had finally been identified and named "Lassa Fever." It started from a severe fever outbreak in the town of Lassa, Nigeria. We also learned that this illness is spread by a certain rat's urine and droppings. We thought right away of Mrs. Moore, who lived in that small house across from us. We sometimes referred to it as "the Mouse House" because of the frequent trapping of mice in that house.

This particular outbreak of Lassa Fever was marked by quick and easy contamination of other persons. At the time, though, it was considered somewhat less virulent in Guinea and neighboring countries of Liberia and Sierra Leone, than it was in Nigeria. Well over a thousand people died in this outbreak, but many more, like me and in God's mercy, were able to recover.

When we returned to the U.S. on home assignment in the summer of 1969, I received a phone call from the CDC in Atlanta, Georgia, informing me that I had the highest-known antibody level in my blood against Lassa Fever, other than Mrs. Moore. They asked me if I would be willing to donate blood so that short-term protective vaccinations could be given to the medical personnel working in the countries dealing with the present outbreak. They even offered to pay me, which, of course, I declined. The CDC made arrangements with a doctor in the hospital in Warren, Pennsylvania, near where we were living at the time.

On the prescribed day, I told Florine I was going to Warren to give some blood. The doctor was waiting for me, and the nurse got me into a bed, found my vein and began to draw blood. The first quantity taken was spun to take out the antibodies and the rest was injected back in through the vein in the other arm, while a second drawing was being done for more antibodies. During this procedure, the doctor was called away, and he left me with his assistant, who found that the blood flow was well increased if he put the container on the floor. Right away the whole hospital room began to spin, and I felt that I was going to pass out or maybe die. "Lord, here I come," I remember praying. Fortunately, the nurse who was monitoring the instruments, told the assistant to stop. When he didn't respond, she reached over and pinched the tube to stop the blood flow.

Things eventually returned to normal, but they wouldn't let me out of bed for an hour. Those were the days before cell phones, and when Florine didn't hear from me, she feared that I had been in an accident. But in spite of all that happened, I felt that the Lord had permitted me to have a part in helping to protect many people from Lassa Fever.

Forty years later, Guinea and surrounding countries were devastated by another outbreak, a highly infectious disease called Ebola, claiming over 11,000 lives in three countries. And now, fifty years later, we are experiencing COVID-19, a pandemic affecting every country in our world. May God spare His people and use this as a means to spread the redeeming gospel of Jesus.

CHILDHOOD FRIENDS

1960 MARKED THE first year of our second term in Guinea and we were stationed in Conakry, the capitol city. The field chairman, Arnold Ratzloff, preferred to live and work in Macenta, while the office in Kankan was run by the secretary, Miriam Cain. I was the business manager in Conakry. Much of my job involved getting visas, putting baggage through customs, meeting travelers, and on Sundays I was the interim pastor of the French Reformed Church in Conakry.

We lived in the house adjacent to the French Reformed Church. It was the last house at the end of a long avenue that came straight out from the center of the city. The thoroughfare made a turn to go around the church property and continued on over a sort of causeway and out of the city proper.

On special occasions, the president of Guinea, Ahmed Sekou Touré, would be driven in his white Cadillac convertible, dressed in a white robe and a white hat, and waving his white kerchief. David was about seven, and he and I would stand at the edge of the street when he went by and wave back at his special wave to us.

The president knew who we were. He and I both grew up in Faranah and as a boy, I played with his younger brother, Ismael. I was the only one in the area that had a bicycle, and Ismael and his friends used to take turns borrowing my bike. They would coast down a hill to this bridge that went over a creek, then come back up the hill and give the bike to the next kid.

When we first arrived in Conakry, I went to meet Sekou Touré, introduce myself and let him know we had moved to the area. He told me he had attended my dad's Sunday School class as a boy at the mission church there.

Years later, in March 1984, I was able to attend Sekou Touré's funeral in Conakry. At the stadium where the funeral was held, I sat near George H. W. Bush, then Vice President, and the American delegation.

CLAIR GOES HOME

MOM AND DAD returned to Guinea in 1949, though not to the Bible school, but to a ministry at Kankan, the mission headquarters. They had been stationed there in the early to mid '20s. My mom started her Bible translation again, working on more Old Testament books. My dad assisted at headquarters and helped with translation when he could. Dad's ministry at Kankan was, in God's plan, cut short.

In June 1950, he was invited to be the speaker for special meetings at the Ntoroso Bible School in neighboring Soudan (now Mali). Dad was driving his new Chevy Suburban, and before he arrived at the Soudan border, he hit a large hole that had been filled with dirt, and was now turned into mud by heavy rain. This whipped the steering wheel from his hands, and the car left the road, hitting a tree and leaving the vehicle not drivable. The accident occurred near a village, and the people there received him. He held a service that night and preached the Gospel to people who may have heard about Jesus for the first time.

He sent a note back to Kankan with a passing truck driver, and the next day Mr. Torgerson, who was a missionary mechanic, brought the mission truck to help. They got Dad's car on the truck and headed back to Kankan. Dad recuperated for several days at home before hopping a public transport truck to head back toward Soudan.

There at the N'Toroso Bible School he spoke to the needs of the students. The last morning Dad spoke with passion about the need for these students to be filled with the Holy Spirit in order to be faithful and effective servants of God. After the service, he returned to the Ernest Howards' home where he was staying, and Eva Howard (a distant cousin) brought him a glass of orange juice. When her knock and a call didn't bring him to the door, she saw through the unlatched door that Dad was lying on the floor. He had passed out, and it was later determined that he had a stroke.

Since the school was out in the "boonies," this created quite an effort to get Dad to a hospital. A telegram to the capital city, Bamako, brought a response from French Colonel Verier, the Director of Security for all French West Africa. He was a believer and a friend of Dad's, and sent an airplane to bring him to Bamako. There was no place for the plane to land, so the plane returned to Bamako, and a telegram instructed the missionaries to clear the vegetation from both sides of a long, straight stretch of road in the area that would permit a small plane to land. This was accomplished by a group of the Bible School students and an MK, Loyal Bowman, whose parents lived there at the Bible School. Loyal is the one who told me the story.

Another smaller plane was sent from Bamako the next day or so, and it was able to land on that section of road prepared for it. Dad was put on the plane on a stretcher, and Dora Bowman, Loyal's mother, accompanied him to the hospital in Bamako. My mother was in Kankan, Guinea, and received a telegram about Dad's evacuation and had only 30 minutes to pack a suitcase and get to the airport to make the last flight to Bamako.

Dad was cared for at the hospital in Bamako for five days. My mother and Dora Bowman both stayed at the hospital with him. Mom told me that Dad always tried to witness to the nurses, speaking to them in Maninka. Because of his stroke, his speech would often become slurred and unintelligible, and she would have to finish telling them about Jesus and His salvation.

Dora Bowman told about one time when she was there on one side of Dad's bed and Mom on the other side. Dad, speaking clearly in Maninka and in his humorous way, said, "Moso fila ka nyin dee!" which interpreted means, "It's great to have two wives!"

Dad passed from his earthly ministry on June 26, 1950, my mother's birthday.

Colonel Verier was a speaker at his funeral. Dad was laid to rest in the large cemetery in the city of Bamako, awaiting the day of resurrection and his eternal reward. At age 54, Dad's life seemed to us to have been cut short, but his vision and ministry had a major impact on the formation and future of the church of Jesus Christ in Guinea. He is remembered in Africa as a strong preacher, teacher and witness of the Gospel of Jesus Christ.

Ruth with translator, Timothy

Clair C. Ellenberger

176

CLAIR C. ELLENBERGER

1896 — 1950

"LE SANG DE JÉSUS SON FILS
NOUS PURIFIE DE TOUT PÉCHÉ."

"The blood of Jesus, his Son, purifies us from all sin."

THE CRAZY MAN

IN THE CITIES, you often run across beggars trying to collect money. They usually beg where people congregate, like at the marketplace. They are usually very poor, suffering some physical deformity, or sometimes a little bit crazy.

One fellow the locals referred to as "the crazy man," was often at the market in Kissidougou, but could be found anywhere in the area. And he might be sleeping on the ground, at the market with people milling all around, or even in the middle of the street sound asleep.

Florine needed something from the market one day, and I drove in to town to get it. Our daughter, Sandie, went along with me for the ride. We arrived at the market to find the crazy man on the ground, fast asleep right where we parked. I told Sandie to remind me when we returned about the sleeping man right in front of our car.

When we got back in the car to leave, Sandie said, "The crazy man!" So I put the car in reverse and started to back away. Just then, a fellow came up to my window to say hello, someone from a nearby village whom I recognized. We talked for a couple of minutes while I kept my foot on the brake. When he left, I instinctively shifted into first gear and started to pull ahead.

There was like a hump I went over, and I hit the brake. Sandie said, "The crazy man!" I couldn't believe that I had just run over him. In shock, I asked Sandie to look out the window to see if she could see him. "I see his legs," she said. "Are they moving?" I asked. "It looks like he's trying to get out from under the car," she said. "Oh, now he's sitting up, rubbing his arm!"

My shock left, and I got out of the car to see the man. He was sitting there on the ground in his few rags, rubbing his arm, which miraculously didn't look broken. I opened the back door of the car to help him in, while the women in the market sitting right there were telling me, "Leave him, leave him. He's crazy!" I replied, "But I've injured him, and I have to take him to the hospital." As I drove away, they were still reminding me that he was crazy.

At the hospital, I checked him in and said that I would be back with clothing and money for his care. But first I had to go to the police station and report the accident. There was no one there, so I drove around until I found a motorcycle policeman that I knew and told him what had happened. "Follow me," he said, as he jumped on his motorcycle and drove to the hospital. He checked everything out, including the money I gave for his food and his room. I promised to bring him some clothes and to see the police chief the next morning.

Amazingly, the crazy man had no broken bones and didn't seem that injured. I went to the hospital every day to see him and to make arrangements for his care. He was living it up – apparently, he had never had it so good! Then I found out that the male nurses at the hospital were actually eating very well, and the crazy man wasn't getting all that I was giving for his care. The police chief said that he was stepping in to get the crazy man released, and driven to another city miles away, so that he would no longer be a local problem.

The police chief had someone take him to a city a longways down the road, and the crazy man returned somehow on his own to Kissidougou before nightfall that very same day! But eventually, time caught up with him. He went to sleep one night in the middle of the paved road there in town, and a truck with poor headlights ran over him. The truck driver and his apprentice took the body and dumped it in a field out of town where the vultures found him.

The chief of police had him buried, and the next time he saw me in town, he told me I wouldn't have to worry about him anymore.

What a sad and disturbing ending to a man's life. Jesus valued all of the people He met and rescued the "crazy man" who lived among the tombs. Perhaps we could have done more to care for the "crazy man" of Kissidougou.

A FAITHFUL HELPMATE

IT WAS THE start of my sophomore year at Houghton College. In my psychology class, I found myself seated alphabetically, beside a very good-looking blonde named Florine Donelson. Not that I was actually looking for a girlfriend, but I kind of liked her.

I found out that she was a music student and was taking psychology as one of her electives. Florine had worked in a factory for two years after high school to pay for college and I had just returned from my Navy service, so we both had a little more life experience than many of the other students. She was a junior at Houghton, as was my younger sister, Dorothy.

Sometime later, I was in a room for extra study one evening where another student was informing the rest of us about his rather long list of female students that he was planning to ask out on dates. When I heard that Florine Donelson's name was on his list, I knew that I would have to move quickly and ask her for a date before this guy got to her. And so I did! And this began a long friendship that blossomed into a true love relationship.

When my parents returned from Africa, they came to Houghton to visit Dorothy and me. Because of my wartime Navy service, I hadn't seen my dad for more than six years and my mother and two brothers for more than five years. My sister and I took them to an evening gathering at the college where we were able to introduce them to our friends.

I introduced Florine to my mother, who I guess didn't know I was dating anyone. She just said, "Glad to meet you." When I told her,

"Mom, you better remember this girl if you don't remember anyone else!" she immediately went to my dad and started pulling on his arm saying, "Clair, you have to meet this girl!" So, Florine was welcomed into the Ellenberger family.

By the time Florine graduated college a year ahead of me, we were engaged. She took a summer course at the State University of New York at Fredonia. Then starting in the fall, she taught first grade at the elementary school in Cuba, New York, not far from Houghton. We got married the following summer, the ceremony performed by Florine's two ordained minister brothers. We spent our honeymoon up in Ontario, Canada, where we rented a cabin at a summer camp.

We both attended the Missionary Training Institute in Nyack, New York, for a year, in preparation for overseas ministry with The Christian & Missionary Alliance. I accepted a call to pastor a small Alliance church in Port Washington, Long Island, New York. Florine led the women's ministry, played the piano for church and also taught piano. We enjoyed our ministry there and learned many lessons that served us well during our years of ministry in Guinea. Two years later, we were asked to go to Guinea, West Africa, as missionaries.

Florine adapted quickly to missionary life in Africa. Her earliest fear that she might have to live in a thatched-roof mud hut was disproved when we arrived in Guinea in early 1955. We were assigned to district work in Faranah, where we lived in a mission-built house with a corrugated metal roof, extra-high ceilings, and thick plastered brick walls. This was the same house I lived in with my parents when I was a kid! We moved to other places and different ministries during our 36-year ministry in Guinea, but we never did live in a hut!

Our first son, David, was born in Port Washington. Our second son, Keith, was born in Africa before our first furlough. Two daughters, Sandie and Karyn, both born in the U. S. on different furloughs, completed our family.

Florine spent a lot of time making dresses for the girls, altering clothes we had purchased in the U.S. and sewing nametags on every item they took to boarding school. She taught the kids how to sew and helped them with piano.

While our 36-year ministry in Guinea required us to perform many different roles, our longest and most effective time were the years we spent at the Telekoro Bible Institute. In addition to raising four children, Florine acted as Hostess for many years. She planned meals and housing, entertaining guests from all over the world. Florine taught many women's classes in the Maninka language, and later taught Bible classes in French. She also taught several students to play the pedal organ, which she played for our church services. One student she helped to learn English, and he later became the Guinea Church president and eventually got his PhD in the United States!

I always wondered why I had not been accepted at Wheaton College the year I wanted to go there. I came to understand that, had I been accepted and attended there, I would not have met Florine. Now I know the Lord put me in the right place at the right time to meet my future wife, a wonderful ministry partner and faithful helpmate.

Studebaker in front of Cabin, Ontario, Canada

184

Church in Port Washington, NY

Florine teaching, Telekoro Bible Institute

Florine playing organ at Telefara Chapel

Our family, circa 1965

A GOODLY HERITAGE

A T OUR MAMOU Foyer boarding school, one of the often-de-
bated issues among the MKs was our heredity. Irish, for some
reason, seemed to be the one that drew the most determined defense.
I had no idea what I was, so I asked my dad. He said, "You're Scotch-
Irish Yankee Doodle Dutch," which seemed a bit long to defend. But,
yes, I was Pennsylvania Dutch. That was a commonly used identity
in Pennsylvania where my paternal grandparents and their families
lived. It was a long time before I realized that it wasn't Dutch, but
Deutsche-German. My dad's ancestors for several generations were
from Germany.

These German immigrants arrived in Pennsylvania between
the late 1600s and the early 1800s. They were basically made up of
Mennonites, as were my ancestors, Amish, Moravian, and other per-
secuted Christian groups seeking freedom of worship in the United
States of America. My cousin, Dick Ellenberger, spent a lot of time
visiting libraries, city halls, and cemeteries in Pennsylvania, in search of
records that would identify our family's history and establish when the
first Ellenbergers came to the U.S. from Germany. He never succeeded,
but as near as he could figure, we were at least eight generations from
the "old country." Eight generations - a "goodly heritage" indeed!

When my father graduated from Nyack Missionary Training
Institute in New York in 1916, he was sent to Toledo, Ohio, for his
pastoral training before going to Africa. His supervisor there was Rev.
Isaac Patterson, pastor of the Toledo Tabernacle of the Christian &

Missionary Alliance. Isaac would later become my dad's father-in-law and my grandfather.

As a young Presbyterian in Ontario, Canada, Isaac Patterson attended a Bible study where he met a young lady, Mary Blair, who would eventually become his wife, and my grandmother. When Isaac felt that the Lord was calling him to the ministry, he went to his pastor for counseling to know what to do. His pastor told him about another Presbyterian pastor, Rev. Albert B. Simpson, who had opened a Bible training school in New York City. He urged Isaac to go to that school.

The school was then called the New York Training Institute, later the Missionary Training Institute, and now Nyack College. Isaac attended this school and graduated in 1893, in the same class with the well-known Alliance pioneer missionary, R.A. Jaffray.

After graduation, Isaac and his fiancé Mary Blair, felt moved to apply for missionary service in China with The Christian & Missionary Alliance, but they were not approved. Mrs. A. B. Simpson, who was on the mission selection board, thought that Isaac looked too weakly to succeed as a foreign missionary.

So, Isaac focused on becoming a pastor. No church seemed to be available in Ontario, but the Reid sisters in southern Ohio heard about him and paid his way to come to their church. Isaac and his new wife moved to Ohio. While pastoring their local church, they learned more about The Christian & Missionary Alliance and were impressed with its focused vision to reach the world for Jesus Christ. Isaac and Mary joined in the effort and over the next few years, planted churches in Columbus, Lima and Toledo, Ohio, before moving to Michigan to establish a church in Flint.

Although my grandparents, Isaac and Mary Patterson, could not go to China as missionaries, they had a long and blessed pastoral ministry in the U.S. They had two daughters (my mother Ruth, and my Aunt Grace) that spent many years as missionaries in West Africa and three grandchildren who also spent many years as missionaries in West Africa (me and my sister, Dorothy) and New Guinea (my brother

John). They had two great-grandchildren (my son Keith, and my niece Patty), and two great-great grandchildren (my grandson, Davin and my grand-nephew, Joshua) who served as overseas missionaries. And Mary Blair Patterson's sister, Helen Elizabeth Blair, my great-aunt, married Rowland Bingham, an early missionary to Central Africa and the founder of the Soudan Interior Mission, now called SIM.

God gave me a good and loving, capable and brave helpmate for our many years in Guinea, West Africa. Florine had three brothers who were life-long pastors and a family with a long Christian heritage.

"Yes, I have a goodly heritage." And I am truly blessed.

The lines are fallen unto me in pleasant places;
yea, I have a goodly heritage.
Psalm 16:6 (KJV)

Rev. Isaac Patterson, Clair's mentor and future father-in-law

192

Clair and Ruth with children: Paul, Dorothy, John and Ralph, circa 1942

Paul and Florrie with 13 grandchildren, 2007

194

FLIGHT TO HONOR

O N THE MORNING of Thursday, April 7, 2016, I was on a plane headed for Washington, DC. This plane was a chartered American Airlines Airbus, designated as a "Flight to Honor." It was loaded with 71 other veterans of WWII, the Korean War and the Viet Nam War. Each veteran was accompanied by a "guardian," and my guardian was my son, Keith.

The flight was coordinated by the Polk County Veterans Council in Florida, to fly veterans to visit the War Memorials in Washington, D.C., as a "flight to honor" them for their service to our country. This entailed raising a significant amount of money. About 300 volunteers donated their time and expertise during a period of nine months to realize this worthy mission. That is impressive!

Our arrival at Reagan National Airport was heralded by water cannons shooting water over the plane as it taxied in along a line of military service flags. Inside the terminal, a band was playing, and a large crowd of people were waving flags and reaching out to shake our hands.

Seventeen of the veterans were in wheelchairs and there were two women veterans from WWII. Many of them had never been to Washington, D.C. before. We visited the World War II Memorial, the Korean War Memorial, the Viet Nam War Memorial, as well as the National Air and Space Museum of the Smithsonian Institution. This was a great thrill for all of us! And everywhere we went, people, even children, wanted to shake our hands and thank us for our service to our country.

A downpour of rain caused a change in plans, so that a scheduled stop at Arlington National Cemetery had to be skipped. The Veterans didn't seem to mind.

On our flight home we were surprised by a "mail call." Each veteran was handed a large manila envelope containing letters, cards, and other messages written by children in different Polk County public schools, as well as those from family and friends. I had 58! How deeply moving it was to read through those messages!

On our arrival back at sunny Lakeland, Florida, our plane was again met with water cannons, a band playing and an enthusiastic crowd of a thousand cheering people outdoors! A double line of uniformed personnel saluted us as we passed, and at the end of the line our loved ones were waiting for us. What a memorable and emotional honoring it was!

Yes, the "Flight to Honor" was an unforgettable experience. But we are reminded that an infinitely more wonderful event awaits us. On that day, we will hear our blessed Savior say to us, "Well done, good and faithful servant . . ."

Paul and Keith, World War II Memorial

197

A SACRIFICIAL COMMITMENT

REMEMBER MY FIRST Easter in an African village with a young pastor. I suggested that we have an outdoor early morning sunrise service to commemorate Jesus' resurrection. The pastor, with some exasperation, said something like, "Why on earth meet outdoors when we have a nice chapel with benches to sit on!"

A few years later, as a Bible Institute teacher, I was invited by a village church to come and be the Easter Sunday morning speaker. Their Easter celebration actually started on Saturday, so I drove out to the village that afternoon in the Mission van so as to be there at least for the evening service. For some unusual reason I was all alone! The village was situated at the top of a rather steep hill with loose dirt on the road, up which my empty van didn't negotiate. I had to back down and try again, but this time the motor conked out. I recognized the problem and got my tools ready to do the necessary repair, which would take me some time, but I would still have to get the empty van up that hill.

Just as I began, I heard the sound of a motor. It was a tractor on its way to the village where I was headed. The driver stopped to check on me and offered to tow me up to the village. With my van now at the village, I was ready to get started on the repair. The driver of a large truck that was parked at the village, came over to see me and offered to do the repair for me. Again, God's provision!

It was just after dark when the van was fixed, and we could hear singing at the church where the evening service had already begun. By the time I got there, the truck driver who had helped me was already at the door listening to the singing. "I've never heard anything like this before," he told me. I invited him in, but he said he had to go. Actually, I never heard his truck motor until after the preaching was done, so he heard a lot that night.

The Easter Sunday morning service was long, but blessed. My message was interpreted, and many responded to the altar call. One man that came forward to pray was someone I recognized, and I went over to pray with him. He was a converted witch doctor. He had had seven wives and had sacrificed four of them to the fetish powers he served. The other three wives ran away! But he heard the Gospel, and like many witch doctors, came to realize that Jesus has more power than his demons do, and he gave his heart to the Lord. He was baptized, took the name of John, the favorite Christian name, married a Christian woman, and became a follower of Jesus.

At the altar that morning, he answered the call to become a dedicated servant of Jesus Christ. He was already a servant of Christ, but in his own heart he felt unworthy because of his past. He understood God's mercy, grace and forgiveness, but felt more comfortabe being a servant of Christ's servants.

For more than two years after this commitment, John went around from church to church in the district helping pastors and pastors' wives, with the most menial service for the Lord. I remember seeing him at work more than once with a baby tied on his back, beating rice in a mortar, both things that in Africa only a woman does. This was John's commitment to the Lord, and he proved faithful.

And the King will answer them, "Truly I say to you, as you did it
to one of the least of these my brothers, you did it to me."
Matthew 25:40

TO GOD BE THE GLORY

WE THANK THE Lord for the many years of ministry He gave us in Guinea, West Africa. Not only did we witness the formation of pastors and workers at the Bible School, but we also played a part in the founding and development of the Church of Jesus Christ in Guinea. We saw the church grow to become a vital spiritual force and an effective witness for Christ in Africa.

As I have re-lived these stories, I am reminded and amazed at God's good hand at work in my life, my family's lives and in the lives of those I have written about. At times we could sense God's providential answer to prayer, but as I reflect on our years in Guinea, I can more clearly recognize God's overall guidance as we participated in carrying out His great commission.

God reminds me continually that He gave me a very special helpmate, my wife Florine, without whom I could never have fulfilled what God gave us to do. And I pray that as you read about what God has done for me – for us – that you will praise Him with us and be encouraged to do great things for Him and in His strength.

It has been a great journey! And we thank our Lord for the many loved ones, friends, fellow workers - His wonderful family - who prayed for us and supported us in our incredible journey of faith. To Him be all the glory!

Saving Goodbye